5 minutes
TO GREAT
REAL ESTATE
MARKETING IDEAS
A DESK REFERENCE FOR TOP-SELLING AGENTS

JOHN D. MAYFIELD

ABR®, ABRM, GRI, e-PRO®, CRB

THOMSON

★

™

SOUTH-WESTERN

Australia · Brazil · Canada · Mexico · Singapore · Spain · United Kingdom · United States

THOMSON

SOUTH-WESTERN

5 Minutes to Great Real Estate Marketing Ideas: A Desk Reference for Top-Selling Agents, 1st Edition
John D. Mayfield

VP/Editor-in-Chief:
Dave Shaut

Executive Editor:
Scott Person

Acquisitions Editor:
Sara Glassmeyer

Developmental Editor:
Arlin Kauffman, LEAP

Sr. Marketing Manager:
Mark Linton

Assoc. Content Project Manager:
D. Jean Buttrom

Manager of Technology, Editorial:
John Barans

Technology Project Manager:
Bryan England

Website Project Manager:
Brian Courter

Manufacturing Coordinator:
Kevin Kluck

Production House:
Pre-Press/PMG, India

Art Director:
Ed Donald

Cover Designer:
Paul Neff

Cover Image(s):
© Getty Images

Printer:
West Group
Eagan, MN

Library of Congress Control Number:
2007906364

For more information about our products, contact us at:

Thomson Learning Academic Resource Center

1-800-423-0563

Thomson Higher Education
5191 Natorp Boulevard
Mason, OH 45040
USA

About John D. Mayfield

John Mayfield received his real estate license at the age of 18 in 1978. John has been a practicing broker since 1981. John was owner and broker of three offices in Southeast Missouri, and managed over 35 real estate agents at one time. John recently sold his real estate company and continues to list and sell real estate on a full-time basis. John has taught pre and post license real estate courses since 1988. John has earned the ABR®, ABRM, CRB, GRI, and e-PRO® designations throughout his real estate tenure.

John is an avid real estate speaker and trainer. John is a Senior GRI instructor for The Missouri Association of REALTORS® and the Arkansas Association of REALTORS® and teaches for the CRB® Council. John has taught thousands of real estate professionals throughout his tenure. He has been a featured speaker at the 2004, 2005 and 2006 National Association of REALTORS® conventions. He is author of four books and creator of the "5 Minute series of real estate books," published by Thomson Learning. John is also one of the contributing editors to the "Sales Coach" section for REALTOR® Magazine Online and is a real estate writer for Hewlett Packard's Web site. John is also very active on a local, state, and national level for the REALTORS® Association and currently serves as NAR Director for the state of Missouri.

John has two children, Alyx and Anne, and he and his wife Kerry own and operate a "Pick Your Own" Blueberry and Blackberry farm in Farmington, MO.

Acknowledgements

It seems like only yesterday that I started the "5 Minute series of real estate books" with Thomson Learning. This is my fifth book with Thomson, and I'm proud to say that I'm still working with the same professional people that I began my journey with some five years ago. To me, that tells a lot about a company to their staff and organization when there is little if any turn over. It also shows their commitment to quality for educational books for the real estate industry, a career that I have spent the better part of my life working in and am so passionate about. For that I say "thank you" to all of my friends and colleagues at Thomson for their hard work and dedication to our industry. Especially "thank you" to Sara Glassmeyer, Mark Linton, Scott Person and Dave Shaut. Without your belief in and commitment to me I would not be where I am today. Thank you Thomson Learning!

I would also like to say thanks to my copy editor Arlin Kauffman for his dedicated and hard work in making sure the finished product turned out as it should. Thank you to everyone at the CRB® Council, including Ginny Shipe, Katie Dwyer, Kristin Carey, Christine Erne, and Marge Helsper. If you're a real estate broker and you are not taking part in the CRB® resources and educational opportunities, you're missing out on some special training! Thanks to Hewlett Packard, Lisa Hopkins, Pam Huss, Arlene Courtney, and all of my good friends there who go above and beyond the call of duty and allow me to write and speak for their great organization. If you have not visited their real estate Web site, then check it out at www.hp.com/go/realestate3. I appreciate and say thank you to my Missouri Association of REALTOR® friends, especially Terry Murphy for writing the forward to this book and for all of her hard work as our educational staff person. Thanks to my own staff and office, especially my two assistants and team members Amanda Gross and Angie Hagerty. You're both the best! Thanks to Active Rain, The Real Estate Tomato, Paul Dizmang, Jessica Hickok, and Paul Pinkston for allowing me to use them in the book.

Finally, thank you to my family members, my Mother Pat Mayfield who introduced me to real estate at the ripe old age of 18, my two daughters Alyx and Anne, and my wonderful wife Kerry, who is always there for me and supports me in every dream and goal I pursue.

Table of Contents

Foreword

5 Minutes to Great Real Estate Marketing Ideas will help you stand out as a unique real estate agent and help you meet the ever-changing real estate needs of today's buyers and sellers. John Mayfield gives you the tools and resources in this book and CD in an easy-to-understand format.

Marketing means different things to different people. Agents face many marketing challenges today: from cost of advertising, printed materials, and strategies, to keeping up with technology and trends. John will show you how to stand out and be different. The real estate industry is very competitive, and you will need to differentiate yourself to survive and thrive in the business. Many home buyers use the Internet as a source of information. An online presence is a must today and needs to be a major component of a real estate professional's marketing strategy.

Each day you have a precious commodity to market—YOU! Don't forget, YOU are valuable and must market your services with integrity to the public, clients, and customers. John will show you how to market yourself effectively and save time. He will help you learn to focus on your key traits and make decisions with ease. You will learn more about the marketing mix, personality traits, and even how to market a hard to sell listing

I have worked with John in different capacities through the Missouri Association of REALTORS®. John continues to shine as a senior GRI instructor as he brings forth new ideas and technology tools to help agents hone their skills in their market, with their clients, and professionally.

I encourage you to use this book and CD in several ways. First, put these great marketing ideas to use right away, whether you implement one or several ideas. Second, communicate with your potential buyers and sellers immediately and build rapport. Third, always respond with enthusiasm. If you are a new agent, build confidence in yourself by using the resources, tips, checklists, and ideas John gives you. If you are a seasoned agent, take your business to the next level and continue a mastery of the profession.

The best part is realizing that, with John's help, you are only 5 minutes to great real estate marketing ideas!

Terry Murphy
e-PRO, GRI
Director of Education
Missouri Association of REALTORS®

Introduction

Welcome to 5 Minutes to Great Real Estate Marketing Ideas. My name is John Mayfield, the creator of the 5 Minute series of real estate books for professionals. I have been a practicing real estate agent for nearly 29 years. This is a career that is close to my heart and one I truly love. After finishing my last book, 5 Minutes to Maximizing Real Estate Technology (an emphasis toward online marketing), I realized the need for a good real estate marketing book. Not a book heavy on marketing theory or practice, but a text that could help implement ideas, programs, action plans, systems, and more for the real estate professional. As I travel across the country teaching real estate agents and meeting top producers, I continue to notice a constant thread that weaves its way in and around successful real estate agents: the need and implementation of "systems!" I hear this same theme over and over from the major real estate producers when asked the question, *"What makes your business successful?"* The answer is always the same: having good systems in place! Establishing and employing a good set of checklists, action plans, and programs to help market and communicate your message on a regular basis is essential for the real estate professional to have a long and prosperous career. 5 Minutes to Great Real Estate Marketing Ideas is a book to help you achieve this goal!

It's easy to forget as a real estate professional how important checklists and action plans are for your business. Your clients are counting on you to communicate on a regular basis actions and completed tasks in a timely manner. Staying in touch with your customers and clients is critical! As real estate agents you have so many functions and to do's on a regular basis that trying or attempting to perform these actions without a system in place is almost impossible.

5 Minutes to Great Real Estate Marketing Ideas is a book to help you put those systems and action plans in place. It contains a collection of letters, flyers, postcards, templates, checklists, and presentation materials that you can use on a daily basis to save time and make more money. Of course, many of the ideas found throughout this book utilize the author's suggested titles, wording, and format, however, as with all of my 5 Minute books, feel free to change and tailor the material to suit your character and personality. After all, it's your real estate career and your customers and clients that you work with on a daily basis. I'm just setting a guide or helping to develop a roadmap for you to use in your real estate career. My hope is that many of the letters and postcards will be easily adaptable or useable in your business without a lot of editing or changing.

The book is broken into sections that describe methods for prospecting for new business, staying in touch with current and past clients and customers, and exploring new ways of marketing your real estate business. All of the materials created in this book have been produced through the HP Real Estate Marketing Assistant Software (REMA) and can be purchased by visiting Hewlett Packard at www.HP.com/Go/RealEstate3. It's the perfect software for creating postcards, letters, and flyers on the go with an easy learning curve that provides you with a professional feel and look. I do want to stress the importance of using

HP papers and products to help maximize your presentation materials and help you stand out above the crowd. Remember, the information you use and how it looks plays a vital role in your image and how the consumer thinks of you early in the sales process. Don't short change yourself by using inexpensive papers or handouts that could give off a negative connotation to your client.

So you have a new listing? Follow the steps as outlined in Chapter 8 to help follow through with the needed tasks, utilizing the materials to communicate to your listing client on a regular basis. Have a closing today? No need to worry, you'll be able to stay in touch with this client for the next few years by letters, postcards and other information through the drip marketing campaign in our after the sale follow-up action plan. Need some ideas for "FREE" reports to generate for inquiries through your Web site or through direct mail pieces you send out? They're here in the book, ready to implement and easy to use for automated implementation from your Web site. Best of all, 5 Minutes to Great Real Estate Marketing Ideas includes a CD-ROM where you can access many of the documents found throughout this book. You'll also find "how to" videos on the CD-ROM where I'll show you how to use the software and other items from the step-by-step videos.

With 5 Minutes to Great Real Estate Marketing Ideas you're now ready to put your real estate business on auto-pilot. Upload many of the documents to Top Producer®, set reminders in Microsoft Outlook, or use your own favorite software that you feel comfortable with. Set dates and times and then merge this information with your contact information so that staying in touch takes only 5 Minutes each and every day. Thank you for purchasing the book, I hope you enjoy it, and, most of all, I trust you'll only be 5 Minutes away from some great real estate marketing ideas!

Best of Luck,
John D. Mayfield

1 The Four P's of Marketing

If you take a marketing class in school, one of the basic principles you will be introduced to is the four P's of marketing. Sometimes this is referred to as the "marketing mix." The four P's are:

- Product
- Price
- Place
- Promotion

To the real estate professional or any service-related or service-oriented industry, for that fact, the marketing mix still applies, but sometimes it can be a little more challenging in applying the four P's in their proper perspectives. Some scholars have converted the four P's into four C's as follows:

- Convenience (Place)
- Cost to the user (Price)
- Communication (Promotion)
- Customer needs and wants (Product)

As you can notice from their descriptions above, the four C's become more customer- or client-oriented in the marketing mix and allow you to be more focused on consumer needs in a service-related industry.

Let's look at the marketing mix as it relates to the real estate professional and focus primarily on the four C's.

Convenience (Place)

Consumers looking for your services will be more apt to use you as a real estate professional if your services are located within a given area that is convenient to their marketplace. Trying to promote your services outside this area would not be a wise decision. Placing signs, digital photos, arranging showings, and presenting offers to someone in a distant location would be difficult if not impossible to achieve on a daily basis.

Convenience can also filter over to the communication aspect of the four C's. For example, what is your Web presence? How easily can today's consumer communicate with you via cell phone, text messaging, blogging, etc.? These are questions the real estate professional must address today to be competitive and effective in the real estate industry.

Costs (Price)

In today's real estate environment, pricing has become a major challenge for real estate professionals. Although pricing has always been negotiable and there have never been set fees in the real estate industry, it has become more common in recent years to see a rise in what is termed "discount" brokerages. Many consumers are looking for the best deal possible, and so costs involved with your real estate services are an important purchasing decision. As with any of the four C's, you, as the real estate agent, can control these factors in the marketing mix and adapt to meet the needs of your marketing base. If you plan to offer a discount brokerage operation, what kinds of services will be included at the cost you will offer? If you plan to offer a more traditional brokerage framework and your fee is set at a higher scale, you will need to inform and explain to consumers why they're paying the difference. One of the most neglected aspects is the real estate professional not explaining the benefits associated with the costs for their services. For example, the following table outlines a sample handout given to clients, detailing the role as a real estate professional, and depicts the value associated with the services provided to the consumer. A blank handout is also available on the CD-ROM included with this book for you to customize for your own listing and marketing presentations.

[Insert Company or Agent Logo Here, Phone, Address, Web Site, Etc.]

Description of Service Offered	Cost ($)
Place property in multiple listing service	21.00
For sale sign	26.00
Advertising in homes guide over a 3 month period	80.00
Advertisement in local newspaper over a 3 month period	125.00
Lock box rental	15.00
Web site hosting and traffic	35.00
Errors and omissions insurance	15.00
Virtual tours	50.00
Secretarial time for adding information to Multiple Listing Service and Web sites	50.00
Postage and postcards to surrounding neighbors	18.00
Agent open house	50.00
Public open house	50.00
Flyer box and flyers kept in box	15.00
Agent time (includes showings, phone calls, and additional time)	500.00
Contracts—disclosures and use of local board forms	100.00
Approximate total of services offered	**1150.00**

It's much easier to defend your charge for fees if you can show the consumer, through the use of a visual in your listing or marketing presentation, what you will be doing for the customer and what fees are associated with these items. I'm sure you can think of many more functions your office provides and additional costs not covered on the form, but this is a good starting point for you to build on. As mentioned earlier, a blank template is available on the CD-ROM for you to construct and use by adding your tasks and functions along with the associated pricing you feel is appropriate.

Communication (Promotion)

One of the biggest challenges for real estate agents is the vehicle of communication as noted under the four C's (which is promotion with respect to the four P's). Real estate professionals must not only promote the products they have for sale (listing inventory) but must also learn to communicate or promote themselves in the buying and selling real estate community. Today, self-promotion is as big a part as the general promoting of houses for sale. For years real estate agents were only concerned with the promoting and advertising of properties they have listed. Today, these marketing endeavors entail promoting not only properties but also the real estate agent's name and attributes to the general buying and selling public. This book places a large emphasis on the communication or promotional aspects of the marketing mix. Many of the letters, promotional pieces, and other information found throughout this book deal primarily with communication and promotional activities of a real estate professional. As noted earlier and can be seen and well-documented of the marketing mix, the factors mentioned are all controllable by you, the real estate professional. The amount of communication or promotion you provide for your marketing career is controlled through the amount of dollars you spend, the number of materials you send out, as well as other activities. Most real estate agents fail to realize that this marketing aspect is controllable and easily managed for success or failure of their careers. Setting up and marketing a proper campaign and following through with consistency and uniformity for building a brand around yourself and your company is important and essential for success in the real estate industry.

Customers Needs and Wants (Product)

You can do all of the communicating in the world, have a convenient location, and supply a reasonable cost to the user, but if you have no product or customer needs and wants for your services, your business will surely fail. It's a strange statement to make as most people in the real estate business feel there is a need for their service or product. Yet many times agents provide this service or suggested need to the general public only to find out later that there is no demand in the marketplace for their service. Still others provide customer needs and wants (product) in a marketplace where the competition is steep and fierce, thus lowering demand with an oversupply of products, which lowers the price in the marketplace. When the income has been reduced as a result of an overabundance of products in the area, it can be difficult to make a profit for yourself. This is where the marketing mix becomes clearer and there results a better understanding as to why the entire marketing mix should be implemented to achieve success. In almost every marketplace there are needs to be fulfilled, but it's your job as a real estate professional to make certain that you're target-marketing the proper needs for your market area.

Summary

In summary, remember that the four P's of marketing play an important role in the success of the real estate professional and in the generation of profit in the real estate industry. Being able to understand how the marketing mix relates to the real estate agent through communicating, cost to consumer, determining the potential market share for needs the consumer wants, as well as making the product convenient for the consumer is important to the real estate agent. These areas weave a necessary mix that helps determine and shape how well your business will perform. Being able to get a good knowledge of the marketing mix as it relates to you as a real estate professional will help move your business forward for many years to come.

2 Who Is Your Market?

Understanding who and where your real estate market is becomes important to the real estate professional. These are the fundamental building blocks for developing and constructing a real estate marketing plan. For example, it would do no good to concentrate your efforts on historic or Victorian homes if there were no supply of or demand for such homes in your marketplace. Nor would it be a wise decision to concentrate on first-time home buyers as a specialty or niche if you were in a marketplace of corporate or executive professionals. The real estate agent who wants to excel and learn more about his or her market always takes time to analyze and evaluate where the greatest percentage of sales are coming from. Looking at comparable homes sold with regard to price, location of sales, and the types of consumers in your marketplace are all important in helping to determine your success as a real estate professional.

Naturally you can obtain a lot of valuable information about your marketplace from your local Multiple Listing Service, as well as information from your local chamber of commerce and/or state and local economic development agencies. Remember, it's always an excellent idea to study and learn your market area to discover where the demand and supply needs are premium!

The S.W.O.T. Theory

Most marketing books and many software programs discuss the implement-tation of the S.W.O.T. theory in building a marketing plan. In other words, what are your strengths, weaknesses, opportunities, and threats (S.W.O.T.) as a real estate professional? The following table will help you implement the S.W.O.T. analysis for yourself. Take a few moments to complete the following table.

S.W.O.T. Analysis

S.W.O.T.	Response
S—Strengths What are some of your strengths as a real estate professional?	
W—Weaknesses Describe some of the weaknesses you have as a real estate professional.	
O—Opportunities Can you spot any opportunities as a real estate professional in your marketplace? If so, describe a niche or specialty marketing real estate expertise that is currently not being employed by another agent.	
T—Threats Are you aware of any threats in your marketplace on a local, state, or national level that could hinder your real estate production during the coming months?	

Use the previous example to help define and build a basis for your real estate marketing campaign you plan to implement.

It's important for you, the real estate professional, in building a marketing plan, to take some time to analyze and evaluate your marketing environment along with your own current business model. Knowing what your needs, wants, and desires are prior to moving forward with your marketing plan is also a critical aspect. Once you've studied your market area and determined the appropriate demand for your product, you're ready to build in the appropriate marketing resources (dollars) for your proposed marketing campaign. Unfortunately many real estate agents miss the mark by not setting the appropriate dollars aside for executing a marketing plan. Generally an annual budget should be developed detailing expenses such as direct mail to your sphere of influence, just listed and sold postcards, advertising, and other marketing dollars to help establish and build an estimated amount for the new year. The following example shows a sample marketing budget for the coming year. The marketing budget template is available on the enclosed CD-ROM. Microsoft Excel is required to run the marketing budget template.

Sample Annual Marketing Budget

Description of Marketing Function	A Monthly Investment	B Number of Times you Plan to Implement Next Year	C Total Investment for Year (A × B)
Postcards for year			
Postage for postcards			
Flyers—letters/stationery			
Postage for flyers			
Advertising in homes magazines			
Local advertising			
Radio advertising			
Web site hosting			
Virtual tours			
Logo—branding start-up costs			
Signs, banners			
Flyer boxes			
Car signs—wraps			
"FREE" items to give away			

Once you've determined the funds you plan to work with for the coming year, you're now able to determine what percentage of your sales must be contributed to pay for your marketing budget.

First, estimate your annual sales you plan to have for the coming year (gross commission income). Next, divide your estimated marketing budget by your projected gross income.

$$\text{Total Marketing Budget} \div \text{Expected Sales} = \text{Percentage to Withhold}$$
$$\$5,000 \div \$50,000 = 10\%$$

Keep in mind that budgets are estimates and targets to shoot for. Sometimes adjustments will need to be made for your budgets based on your year-to-date sales and potential forecasts with the economy. However, beginning this process will help you move in the right direction for your marketing campaign.

Summary

It's important to remember that for any successful marketing plan or campaign to exist you must first know and have a niche for your market area. Take the time to evaluate and study the area to see where these needs are. Next, perform the S.W.O.T. analysis on your current business. A S.W.O.T. analysis will help you determine where your strengths, weaknesses, opportunities, and threats lie in your real estate career. Finally, be sure to develop a marketing budget for your real estate business. Plan for the dollars you'll need to execute this marketing campaign. Once you've developed an annual marketing budget, you'll then need to estimate your gross income for the year that you've set as a goal. By performing a few quick mathematical functions you'll arrive at a percentage of income to withhold from each commission check earned to fund your annual marketing budget.

3 For-Sale-by-Owners (FSBOs)

Introduction

As a real estate professional, the lifeblood of your business is listings! I've used this phrase a lot at many training seminars—"listing is existing!" Without houses to sell or buyers to work with, you have no products! As in any business, having the right inventory can make all of the difference in the world. "One good prospecting idea is for the real estate professional to work with for-sale-by-owners (FSBOs)." Or better yet: "One good prospecting idea involves the real estate professional working with for-sale-by-owners (FSBOs)." This type of marketing is not exciting for many real estate agents. After all, there's a certain amount of fear in contacting someone you don't know—fear of rejection and failure and the simple worry that you might disrupt or discourage the potential prospect. However, the FSBO is an excellent market to pursue if done correctly as a real estate agent. The main purpose and objective when dealing with FSBOs is to develop and maintain a friendship. Remember your goal with contacting a FSBO is *not* to get the listing on the first attempt. You're one of many real estate agents inquiring about the property. Your job is to be different from the other agents. Building trust and a friendship is essential if you want to win the listing from the FSBO! Keep this goal in mind as you work the FSBO prospect.

The second objective when dealing with the FSBO is to have a plan of action! Many professionals will attempt to call the FSBO only once or twice. If there's no immediate reaction, they will normally give up easy. This is why so many real estate agents end their pursuit of the FSBOs. Keep in mind that it may take as many as six to ten attempts or contacts before you will have any success with most prospects, including the FSBO. Therefore, having a game plan and a strategic process of how you will make contact with the FSBO without aggravating or wearing out your welcome is important.

Your third objective with an FSBO is to make sure you conform to all necessary codes of ethics, standards of protocol, rules and regulations, and your company policy and procedures when contacting this group of customers. It's important that you follow all of the "do not call" laws and that you follow a strict code of conduct so that no rules or laws are broken when attempting to work the FSBO market.

Make calling on the FSBO fun and enjoyable. If this is not an area you enjoy for prospecting, then choose another method in the book and use it to help build your business. Keep in mind that you will need to implement some type of prospecting method if you want to succeed in the real estate industry.

Who Is the FSBO?

Understanding the FSBO motivation prior to beginning your action plan for prospecting this type of clientele is helpful. Most FSBOs have one goal in common when it comes to selling on their own and that's "saving the commission"! The following table illustrates some interesting facts about why FSBOs want to go for it alone.

Reason to Sell on Own	2004 (%)	2005 (%)	2006 (%)
To save from paying a commission	61	53	51
Because the seller knew the buyer	17	22	22
Because the buyer contacted the seller	9	9	12
The seller did not want to work with an agent	6	8	8
The seller was already a licensed real estate agent	2	2	2
The agent could not sell their home	2	3	3
Seller could not find a real estate agent	1	N/A	1
Other reasons not noted	2	3	2

This information was obtained from the National Association of REALTORS® (NAR) Profile of Buyers and Sellers, 2004, 2005, 2006 editions, NAR Research.

As you can notice from the table, most sellers want to sell on their own to save the commission; however, a growing number of sellers are now becoming FSBOs because they know the buyer. This is a good indication that with many or most of your FSBO materials and your presentation to FSBOs, you must show your value or worth as a real estate agent. If the FSBO wants to save on commission, they need to know how you as a real estate agent can either save them money or that you're worth the money. Research shows that most FSBOs earn "less" money when they attempt it alone. According to the data from the NAR Profile of Buyers and Sellers, 2006 edition, FSBO homes sell for 25% less than agent-assisted homes. This is an important piece of information that should be incorporated into your presentations and materials you distribute to FSBOs.

The Game Plan

Let's develop a game plan to use when working with FSBOs in your day-to-day business. First off, remember that this is only a suggested game plan, and your ideas and thoughts may differ from those listed in this section. Feel *free* to tailor the Microsoft Excel spreadsheet to meet your style and personality. You will find this spreadsheet on the enclosed CD-ROM to use with your prospecting and working the FSBO market.

   Take some time to review these suggestions and list any additional methods of communication you would like to implement with this game plane.

FSBO Game Plan

Week	Action	Completed √
First	Call or personal visit to the FSBO	☐
Second	Follow-up with a thank you card	☐
Third	Postcard #1	☐
Fourth	Postcard #2	☐
Fifth	Call or visit	☐
Sixth	Prepare market analysis	☐
Seventh	Postcard #3	☐
Eighth	Postcard #4	☐
Ninth	Call or visit	☐
Tenth	Sample Flyer—Letter	☐
Eleventh	Call or visit	☐
Twelfth	Postcard #5	☐
Thirteenth	Postcard #6	☐
Fourteenth	Call or visit	☐
Fifteenth	Final letter	☐
Sixteenth	Final call or visit	☐

See the appendix at the end of the book for examples of postcards and flyers to be used with prospecting various consumer groups.

Sample Dialogues

Here are some sample scripts you might want to take time to study and memorize or implement in your own fashion:

1. We have a friend in the real estate business!

"First of all, thank you for letting me know about your friend in the real estate business. Can I ask you if they're a full-time or part-time agent?" Remind the FSBO that, if there are personal issues they do not want to share with their friend, you could still handle the transaction and pay their acquaintance a referral fee. Don't discourage the use of their friend; only remind them that you can be a disinterested party who can be open and honest with them during the home-selling process.

2. We have had a lot of showings on our own!

Congratulate them on the many lookers, but remind them that many of the potential buyers may not be qualified. Encourage them to be careful and let them know that from a security standpoint it might not be good to have too many strangers looking at their property. Security is a major point to make the FSBO aware of.

3. We had our property listed before and had no showings from the other agent.

This is a good time to remind sellers that you too have clients that you have not shown their property to. Explain that you only show qualified buyers who are sincere about purchasing real estate. Use the security issues here too.

4. We owe so much money that we need to save the commission.

This is a good time to share statistics regarding how many home sellers sell their properties for less money than what they are really worth. This is a good time to ask if you could do a Comparable Market Analysis so that the sellers would know firsthand what your thoughts and feelings are regarding the price. Be sure and give the FSBO a true and honest picture of what you think their home is worth. Giving an inflated price to make the seller like you is wrong and will do nothing to help encourage or build your character.

5. We think we may have someone interested who might come back and write an offer.

Many times buyers will tell FSBOs that they will go to the bank to check on their money, only using this statement to avoid hurting the seller's feelings. It might be beneficial if your agency allows you to take listings with an exclusion for a short period of time. Make sure your office allows this type of listing. If the exclusion comes back in a short period of time, you will let them sell at little or no commission due.

Keep in mind that whatever the objection it can be overcome by the right answer and displayed with good confidence.

6. We just started marketing our property last week and want some time to sell it on our own.

Don't discourage the FSBO from doing this. Everyone wants to try this, and normally they will not have good luck marketing the property on their own. Remember your first goal—make a friend and build a relationship. Remind yourself that many other agents will only make one or two contacts. If you can build a relationship and stay in communication with the FSBO, you will be first in line to get the listing.

Practicing scripts and dialogues is important to help you build confidence and to display a professional image to the potential client. Contacting FSBOs can be a fun and rewarding experience and will lead to a good business stream if practiced correctly.

This idea to use with FSBOs is a handy tool for contacting these potential clients without violating the "do not call" list. Purchase a small white box from your local office supply store. Attach a label as shown in the following figure:

The following is a list of items you might consider using with your FSBO tool kit. Although this is not a complete list of items to include in your tool kit, it will help you in providing information to the potential client, creating a friendship, and beginning the process of building trust and faith in the consumer.

- Sample sales contract
- Sample sellers disclosure
- Sample lead-based-paint disclosure
- Home warranty brochure
- Agent resume
- Company resume
- Introductory letter
- Information about the Multiple Listing Service
- Company and agent Web site information
- Testimonials from satisfied clients
- Your commitment to clients
- Sample flyer

- Sample postcard
- A copy of a *free* report (list at end of chapter)
- Graphs or charts regarding how homes are sold
- Information about FSBO homes selling for less money than when agent assisted
- Important facts and details about you or your company sales statistics
- A few "*free*" nominal promotional items

It's important that once you've made contact with the FSBO you stay in touch with the prospect on a "regular" basis. Don't badger or bug the potential client, but do stay in touch and build your friendship as discussed throughout the chapter.

The following pages contain some sample letters that you may consider implementing throughout your FSBO action plan for staying in touch with the prospect. You can also find more letters in my best-selling book, *5 Minutes to a Great Real Estate Letter,* published by Thomson Learning.

509 East Main St.
Park Hills, MO 63601
Office: 573-756-0077
Cell: 573-760-4220 Fax: 573-756-1336
Email: John@RealEstateTechGuy.com
Website: www.RealEstateTechGuy.com

We're Not #1, You Are!

[Date]

«Address Block»

«Greeting Line»

Hello, my name is *[letter name]* and I am associated with *[company name]*. While traveling through your neighborhood today I noticed that you had your home for-sale-by-owner. You have a nice looking home that has excellent curb appeal, and I am certain you will have no trouble selling your real estate in a timely manner if it is priced correctly. I have an excellent report that I would love to share with you entitled *"10 Mistakes Every For Sale By Owner Should Avoid."* This report is *free* and is available by calling me at *[agent's phone number]*.

If you are thinking about purchasing another home locally after the sale of your residence, I would love to help you find a new home. I could set up a detailed computer search on the type of property you desire for your next home. Once new listings become available in our Multiple Listing Service, I can share those with you so that you will be one of the first to hear about these new listings. This service is *free* and requires no obligation or commitment on your part.

I appreciate your time. I wish you the best of luck in selling your home, and if I can help you in any way or if you would like to have my *free* report on the *"10 Mistakes Every For Sale By Owner Should Avoid,"* please feel free to call or write me today. You can reach me at *[agent's phone number]* or e-mail me at *[e-mail address]*. You can also view all of my listings online at *[agent's Web address]*.

Again thanks for your time, and I hope to hear from you soon!

Sincerely,

[Agent's Name]
[Agent's Title]

509 East Main St.
Park Hills, MO 63601
Office: 573-756-0077
Cell: 573-760-4220 Fax: 573-756-1336
Email: John@RealEstateTechGuy.com
Website: www.RealEstateTechGuy.com

We're Not #1, You Are!

[Date]

«Address Block»

«Greeting Line»

I noticed you have your home for sale, and I wanted to compliment you on such an aggressive marketing campaign. Most for-sale-by-owners fail to include flyer boxes in their front yard with information for prospective buyers. I feel it's a great challenge and opportunity for all sellers to market their own property, but I also realize that many sellers at some point turn their services over to a real estate company. Should you come to that point where you would need the services of a real estate agency, I would like to share some of my marketing strategies and successful results. In the meantime, to show my appreciation for you taking the time out to read my letter, I would like to make available 25 *free* copies (color or black and white) of your marketing flyers when you run out. To take advantage of this *free* offer, you will need to contact me directly at *[agent's phone]*. It is a small token of appreciation on my part for you allowing me the opportunity to meet you and help you during the sale of your property.

If you would like to find out more about my company or my services in advance, you can visit my Web site at *[agent's Web site address]*. As always, thank you for your time, and I hope you have a great day! Call me any time for your *free* copies.

Sincerely,

[Agent's Name]
[Agent's Title]

509 East Main St.
Park Hills, MO 63601
Office: 573-756-0077
Cell: 573-760-4220 Fax: 573-756-1336
Email: John@RealEstateTechGuy.com
Website: www.RealEstateTechGuy.com

We're Not #1, You Are!

[Date]

«Address Block»

«Greeting Line»

I was driving through your neighborhood today and noticed your home for sale on *[street name]*. I am sure that you are aware that most homes in your neighborhood are selling for top dollar and that the time a home spends on the market is relatively short. I would be happy to provide you with a *free* statistical report from our Multiple Listing Service on what homes are selling for in your neighborhood as well as the average days on the market. This report is based on other properties similar to yours that have sold in the last year. To accurately provide this report to you, I would need to know just a few pieces of information about your property. We could either do this by telephone or we could make an appointment for me to visit your property in person, whichever is convenient for you.

Why would you need a marketing analysis or a statistical report from me? Sometimes for-sale-by-owners may have an interested buyer who is still uncertain about the price you are asking. Having a market analysis and other statistical data available can help solidify your rationale and reasoning for the price you have suggested. After all, it is a proven fact that information in writing, which can be read and seen, is more believable than the spoken word. Again this information and statistical research is provided to you at no cost and available by a quick phone call. Call me *[agent's name]* at *[agent's phone number]* to get your *free* statistical research on what homes are selling for in your neighborhood.

I appreciate your time. I look forward to hearing from you soon, and I wish you the best of luck with the sale of your property!

Sincerely,

[Agent's Name]
[Agent's Title]

509 East Main St.
Park Hills, MO 63601
Office: 573-756-0077
Cell: 573-760-4220 Fax: 573-756-1336
Email: John@RealEstateTechGuy.com
Website: www.RealEstateTechGuy.com

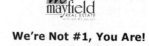

We're Not #1, You Are!

[Date]

«Address Block»

«Greeting Line»

Did you know that most for-sale-by-owners lose money? I don't mean to be blunt or callous with you by making such a frank statement, but research has shown that most for-sale-by-owners do not get the proper amount of money for their property. If you feel you may not be getting an adequate and accurate price for your property, I would love to help you. I would be more than happy to provide a *free* comparable market analysis on what your property is worth on today's market. This report is provided to you at no cost and no obligation and will show you exactly what I, as a real estate professional, think your property would sell for should it be listed with a real estate agency. This report is also beneficial for you to show prospective buyers as they visit your home, helping to strengthen your argument on why you are asking the price you are. It is also a great opportunity for you to possibly get more money for your real estate should that be the case.

If you have an interest in this *free* report and would like more information about my statistical research, please feel *free* to contact me *[agent's name]* at *[agent's phone number]*. I appreciate your time, and I look forward to hearing from you soon.

Sincerely,

[Agent's Name]
[Agent's Title]

509 East Main St.
Park Hills, MO 63601
Office: 573-756-0077
Cell: 573-760-4220 Fax: 573-756-1336
Email: John@RealEstateTechGuy.com
Website: www.RealEstateTechGuy.com

We're Not #1, You Are!

[Date]

«Address Block»

«Greeting Line»

Myth or fact? Selling your home on your own can save you thousands of dollars. Although many sellers feel that selling their home on their own can be a financial savings, in reality many times a for-sale-by-owner will lose money going this road alone. Hi, my name is *[agent's name]* with *[agency's name]* and I wanted to share with you some reasons why selling your home on your own may not be the right decision. Although I appreciate and admire you for tackling this complicated process, I do feel that you should be aware of some of the dangers and pitfalls in selling your home on your own. I have enclosed a *free* report entitled *[free report here]* for you to have and review.

If you would be interested in visiting with me regarding any real estate questions you might have in selling your home, please feel *free* to call. You can reach me at *[agent's phone number]* or e-mail me at *[agent's e-mail address]*. To show my appreciation to you for taking time out of your busy schedule to read my letter and *free* report, I am offering you a special opportunity to receive a *free* marketing flyer and 25 *free* copies to hand out to potential buyers that may stop by. To take advantage of this *free* offer, you will need to contact me directly at *[agent's phone number]*. This offer is only valid while your house is not listed with another firm.

I appreciate your time, and I wish you the best of luck in selling your home, and I hope to hear from you soon regarding your *free* marketing flyer and your 25 *free* copies.

Sincerely,

[Agent's Name]
[Agent's Title]

509 East Main St.
Park Hills, MO 63601
Office: 573-756-0077
Cell: 573-760-4220 Fax: 573-756-1336
Email: John@RealEstateTechGuy.com
Website: www.RealEstateTechGuy.com

We're Not #1, You Are!

[Date]

«Address Block»

«Greeting Line»

Do you know how most homes are sold today? According to the National Association of REALTORS® and many other research projects, the majority of homes are sold today through the Multiple Listing Service! That's right, buyers working with other real estate agents normally find their properties from real estate professionals searching the Multiple Listing Service. When your property is listed with a real estate agent who is a member of the Multiple Listing Service, your property is exposed to a wide variety of real estate agents from the *[insert area]*. Whether you choose to list your property with my firm or someone else's, make sure the real estate firm is a member of the Multiple Listing Service. This is a critical and key piece of marketing efforts you should employ. At *[agency's name]*, we're proud to be members of the *[Multiple Listing Service name]*, and we would love to help you market your real estate through our local Multiple Listing Service and through our Internet presence.

If you would like more information on how your property could be promoted through our local Multiple Listing Service and to get the aid of all the local Multiple Listing Service members working to sell your real estate, contact me *[agent's name]* at *[agent's phone number]* today. I appreciate your time and look forward to hearing from you soon, and I thank you for taking time out of your busy schedule to read my letter.

Sincerely,

[Agent's Name]
[Agent's Title]

509 East Main St.
Park Hills, MO 63601
Office: 573-756-0077
Cell: 573-760-4220 Fax: 573-756-1336
Email: John@RealEstateTechGuy.com
Website: www.RealEstateTechGuy.com

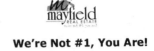

We're Not #1, You Are!

[Date]

«Address Block»

«Greeting Line»

Don't go nuts trying to sell your home on your own! I know how crazy and wild it can sometimes be marketing your own property, and believe me it is just as difficult sometimes as a real estate professional in selling a parcel of real estate. But overall it can be a rewarding and self-gratifying experience. I admire you and commend you on taking such an opportunity to market your real estate on your own, and based on the curb appeal of your property from my drive by, I feel certain you will be able to sell your home quickly. As a small token of my appreciation I have included a bag of peanuts compliments of *[agent's name]*. When and if you get ready to interview real estate agents, I would love an opportunity to talk to you about the marketing of your real estate. You can contact me at *[agent's phone number]* anytime.

Again, *"don't go nuts"* trying to sell your own home; let me help! Thank you for your time, and I look forward to hearing from you soon. I hope you enjoy the peanuts!

Sincerely,

[Agent's Name]
[Agent's Title]

509 East Main St.
Park Hills, MO 63601
Office: 573-756-0077
Cell: 573-760-4220 Fax: 573-756-1336
Email: John@RealEstateTechGuy.com
Website: www.RealEstateTechGuy.com

We're Not #1, You Are!

[Date]

«Address Block»

«Greeting Line»

While meeting some clients this morning in your neighborhood, I noticed your home for sale and wanted to give you my *free* report retain "on" *"10 Mistakes Every For-Sale-By-Owner Should Avoid."* I understand your desire to market your property on your own, and I am sure you are finding many of the obstacles I face as a real estate professional on a daily basis. Although selling real estate can be a rewarding and satisfying experience, it can also pose many problems and issues if you are not fully prepared. I believe you will find this *free* report that I am offering you a real benefit in facing and overcoming many of the challenges of a for-sale-by-owner.

Please know that as a full-time real estate professional I am available to assist sellers like you with the daily problems and concerns that arise and would love to be of assistance to you with your real estate needs. Any time you would like to schedule a *free* consultation on tips or marketing ideas to help sell your home quickly, I would love to assist you. You may contact me at *[agent's phone number]* any time that is convenient for you.

I appreciate you taking time out to read my letter, and I hope we can visit soon regarding your real estate needs.

Sincerely,

[Agent's Name]
[Agent's Title]

509 East Main St.
Park Hills, MO 63601
Office: 573-756-0077
Cell: 573-760-4220 Fax: 573-756-1336
Email: John@RealEstateTechGuy.com
Website: www.RealEstateTechGuy.com

We're Not #1, You Are!

[Date]

«Address Block»

«Greeting Line»

Have you ever wondered what the ten best tips are for selling your home smoothly in today's marketplace? I have a *free* report that I would be happy to share with you entitled *"10 Tips for Selling Your Home Smoothly."* This brief report is full of great ideas on how to sell your home fast! For a *free* copy of this report please contact me, *[agent's name]*, at *[agent's phone number]*. I am also happy to share this report via e-mail. The contact e-mail address for this report is *[tensellertips@yourdomain.com]*.

Thank you for taking time out to read my letter. I hope you will call or write to me about my *free* report, and I look forward to visiting with you soon.

Sincerely,

[Agent's Name]
[Agent's Title]

509 East Main St.
Park Hills, MO 63601
Office: 573-756-0077
Cell: 573-760-4220 Fax: 573-756-1336
Email: John@RealEstateTechGuy.com
Website: www.RealEstateTechGuy.com

We're Not #1, You Are!

[Date]

«Address Block»

«Greeting Line»

I noticed your house for sale today while driving through your subdivision, and I wanted to provide you with two quick tips that I feel are beneficial for every for-sale-by-owner.

1. **Cover your information!** It is important as a for-sale-by-owner that you have all of the information available for potential buyers. For example, copies of your real estate taxes, a plat or survey of your lot, a detailed sellers disclosure statement, and an average monthly utility bill are all beneficial items to have available and in place in case a potential purchaser asks for this information.

2. **Don't give away the farm!** Remember that buyers looking at your property will be paying close attention to your remarks and comments. Sometimes sellers can give away too much information, which can go against them later on during the negotiating process. Although you want to be open and friendly with your dialog, try not to sound overanxious.

As a real estate professional I am always available to help for-sale-by-owners, buyers, and other consumers with their real estate needs. This is just a small token of my appreciation for your time, and to ask your consideration to invite me at a later date to present my full marketing plan should you decide to use the services of a real estate professional.

I appreciate your valuable time and I thank you for taking time out to read this information, and I hope you found it a benefit and help with the marketing of your property.

Sincerely,

[Agent's Name]
[Agent's Title]

509 East Main St.
Park Hills, MO 63601
Office: 573-756-0077
Cell: 573-760-4220 Fax: 573-756-1336
Email: John@RealEstateTechGuy.com
Website: www.RealEstateTechGuy.com

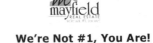

We're Not #1, You Are!

[Date]

«Address Block»

«Greeting Line»

While traveling through your neighborhood today, I noticed your home for sale. I am sure you have been bombarded by many real estate agents asking for your business. Yes, I too would love to be of assistance in helping you sell and market your property, but my letter is for a different purpose. Normally most people who sell their property are also in the market to purchase a new home. This new home could be local, across town, even across state, or in another part of the country. Regardless of where your new home purchase might take you, I would love to be the real estate agent you choose to help find your new home. I have access to the newest listings through our Multiple Listing Service and would be happy to put you on a computerized mailing list so that you would find out about these new homes the minute they are available. I can also arrange for a colleague to help with your real estate services even if the home purchase takes you miles away from our location. As a member of the National Association of REALTORS® *[any other affiliations or associations you prefer]* I have access to other highly trained real estate professionals who can assist in providing you information about their local real estate market, schools, and other information you might request.

Again, I would love to help you in the marketing of your current property to ensure a smooth and quick sales transaction, but please keep me in mind for the purchase of your new home or with help in finding properties for your future destination. You can contact me by phone at *[agent's phone number]* or e-mail at *[agent's e-mail]*. I appreciate your time; I hope you have a great day, and I look forward to hearing from you soon.

Sincerely,

[Agent's Name]
[Agent's Title]

509 East Main St.
Park Hills, MO 63601
Office: 573-756-0077
Cell: 573-760-4220 Fax: 573-756-1336
Email: John@RealEstateTechGuy.com
Website: www.RealEstateTechGuy.com

We're Not #1, You Are!

[Date]

«Address Block»

«Greeting Line»

Are you relocating to another area outside of *[area name]*? If so, I can be of assistance in helping you find a highly trained and successful real estate agent for your destination. I can also assist with gathering information on schools, hospitals, parks, and recreational activities for your future location. Please feel *free* to contact me at *[agent's phone number]* or send me an e-mail at *[agent's e-mail address]*.

Oh, by the way, if you need help with marketing your current property to get the maximum amount of money in the shortest time frame possible, I can help with that too! I have some proven marketing techniques and strategies that have been successful for many of my clients as well as a fully functional Internet Web presence that many buyers access to find properties for sale in our area. I have enclosed my agent resume with this letter, and I am available to answer any other questions you might have by phone. Best of all, there is no pressure and no obligation to list!

Again, thank you so much for taking time out of your busy schedule to read my letter, and please let me know if I can help you find information on properties or the community that you might be relocating to. I look forward to hearing from you soon.

Sincerely,

[Agent's Name]
[Agent's Title]

509 East Main St.
Park Hills, MO 63601
Office: 573-756-0077
Cell: 573-760-4220 Fax: 573-756-1336
Email: John@RealEstateTechGuy.com
Website: www.RealEstateTechGuy.com

We're Not #1, You Are!

[Date]

«Address Block»

«Greeting Line»

Does completing the forms scare you? According to the National Association of REALTORS®, most for-sale-by-owners worry more about completion of the paperwork than anything else when selling their property. Although this is a major obstacle for many for-sale-by-owners, it can be handled effectively and with little ease by hiring an attorney or a real estate agent like me for a reduced fee. Our company will work with for-sale-by-owners at a reduced fee if you find the purchaser on your own. If you are interested in finding out more about how I can assist your paperwork and the completion of the necessary forms to make your transaction run smoothly when you find a buyer, call me, *[agent's name]*, at *[agent's phone number]*.

Completing and filling out the forms does not have to be something to worry about anymore with our new for-sale-by-owner marketing assistance program. Call me at your earliest convenience and I will be glad to explain all the details. Thank you for taking time out of your busy schedule to read my letter, and I look forward to hearing from you soon.

Sincerely,

[Agent's Name]
[Agent's Title]

509 East Main St.
Park Hills, MO 63601
Office: 573-756-0077
Cell: 573-760-4220 Fax: 573-756-1336
Email: John@RealEstateTechGuy.com
Website: www.RealEstateTechGuy.com

We're Not #1, You Are!

[Date]

«Address Block»

«Greeting Line»

While driving through you neighborhood today, I noticed that your home was up for sale. I am sure by now you've been experiencing some of the same joys and sorrows that I experience on a daily basis as a real estate professional. I have a copy of a *free* report entitled *"10 Mistakes Every For Sale By Owner Should Avoid."* This report will be a big help to you in selling of your real estate and is available by contacting me at *[agent's phone number]* or e-mailing me at *[fsbooffer@yourwebsiteaddress.com]*.

I wish you the best of luck in the marketing of your real estate, and should any questions or concerns arise during this real estate transaction process, I would be happy to assist (provided it is in my legal jurisdiction). Thank you for your time, and please let me know if you would like a copy of this *free* report mailed or e-mailed to you. I hope you have a great day!

Sincerely,

[Agent's Name]
[Agent's Title]

The following pages contain some *"free"* reports that can be used for prospecting with the FSBO. You can offer these reports through advertisements in local newspapers, homes magazines, or from your Web site. Many agents find *"free"* reports helpful in generating leads from consumers who may be considering buying or selling in the near future. You might also have a page built on your Web site where these reports can be accessed by submitting an e-mail and other personal information. By doing this you will obtain valuable information from your prospects for communicating with them on a regular basis via e-mail.

Please feel *free* to add or change any information to the reports that suits your needs or applies to your geographical area. As with the letters, you will find copies of the *"free"* reports on the CD-ROM, which is accessible in Microsoft® Word 2003 or earlier.

Five Must Do's Every FSBO Must Know

1. Remember to put away valuables and lock up expensive personal belongings, even if most people looking at your home to purchase are likely to be legitimate home buyers. Some people may be on the prowl to see what you have. Make sure you don't provide any type of opportunity to the wrong person to see items of interest.

2. Have the proper forms ready to go. You are selling your home on your own, and it is important to remember that some buyers are ready to buy on the spot, and if you wait too long, the interest could go down and buyer remorse could set in. If you are planning on being an FSBO, you need to be ready with the proper forms completed and signed so that your potential buyer can be locked in place before they find another property. Make sure your attorney prepared the sellers' disclosure, contract for sale, and lead-based-paint addendum if your home was built prior to 1978, along with all of the other state and local disclosure and form requirements.

3. Don't lock yourself into contingencies issues the buyer might have. Most contracts normally have contingency clauses and paragraphs for the buyer. For example, how long do they have to apply for a loan? How long do they have to get loan approval? Is the contract contingent upon the sale of another home and if so, how long is the other home under contract? These are all areas you should research and investigate prior to signing any legal document prior to locking yourself into a lengthy contract and possible loosing another qualified good purchaser.

4. Complete a seller's disclosure in advance. Although this may not be a requirement in every state or local municipality, it is a good idea to provide the potential buyer with a detailed seller's disclosure about your home. Make sure that you have the proper forms prepared by your attorney and completed in an honest and detailed manner so that there is no chance the buyers could come back at a later date requesting you to correct or repair.

5. Have a detailed marketing flyer placed in a flyer box outside your property. Sometimes good prospects will drive by your home with and interest or unwell to call or notify you if you are working with an agent. It only makes sense that most real estate agents will be promoting or pushing properties they have listed as that is their fiduciary obligation and will avoid FSBOs as there is a fear that they may not be paid a fee if that is the home the

buyer chooses. By having a flyer out front, you can encourage potential prospects to stop and pick up a marketing brochure that might entice them further to call you to look at your home.

Ten Mistakes Every FSBO Should Avoid

1. Drafting the real estate contract on your own. Although you may be tackling the challenge to sell your property on your own, regarding the marketing, showing, and negotiating details while also trying to do the legal side of the real estate transaction is something most FSBOs should avoid. It is always good practice to hire an attorney to help with your real estate contract if a real estate professional is not involved in the transaction.

2. Failing to provide the potential buyer with a seller's disclosure. Normally most real estate transactions involve a detailed disclosure provided by the seller to the buyer outlining minor and major issues regarding the real estate that is being sold—such as mechanical and structural defects that have occurred over the owner's ownership. Some courts have determined that, if particular items are not disclosed to the buyer, a contract could be resented or monetary damages could result to the previous owner. Naturally, only a court of law can make these determinations, and it is good practice to provide a seller's disclosure any time you are selling a property. Consult your attorney for this form if you choose not to hire a real estate professional for this transaction.

3. Failing to provide the federal lead-based-paint disclosure documentation. If your property was built before 1978 (in certain circumstances for properties built during the year 1978), then you're required to provide a lead-based-paint disclosure to the buyers. Failing to do so could result in legal consequences. Consult your attorney for this form if you choose not to hire a real estate professional for this transaction.

4. Neglecting to register all potential buyers who preview your property. Although everyone that comes to look at your home may appear and seem to be a potential buyer, in reality and unfortunately some people previewing you property have more in mind than buying your home. It is always a good idea to make note or register potential buyers along with their license plate numbers, and other details in case a problem occurs after the sale, such as a theft or loss of personal property.

5. Providing too much information. Although many sellers know how much money they have invested in their property and believe that is a good selling feature to provide to potential buyers, sometimes giving too much information during the showing of the property can make it appear as though you're desperate or that something is wrong with the real estate.

6. Failing to disclose material defects. Failing to disclose a material defect in the property can become a major liability in the future after the sale. If you know any major defects in the property, structural, mechanical or other issues, or items that you feel the buyers should know about, then it must be disclosed! Always disclose all material defects in the property.

7. Pricing your property incorrectly. Even though most FSBOs want to sell their property because they can save the marketing fee that a real estate brokerage charges, studies have indicated that most FSBOs end up selling their property for less money than what it is actually worth on today's market. Even though you may be planning on selling the property on your own, it is always a good idea to have an independent appraiser or two or three real estate brokers offer you a price opinion so that you can feel confident that your property is priced accurately.

8. Most FSBOs are not used to negotiating price and other items during the real estate transaction. Understanding important issues such as earnest money, possession, loan commitment, and inspection dates can all play a major role in negotiating a sales contract. Understanding what items can be negotiated for more or in better terms is something the FSBO should take into consideration.

9. Understanding contingencies. As an FSBO, it may sometimes be easy to get an offer to purchase on your property. However, what kind of contingencies have been placed in the verbiage of the contract? How quickly must the buyers get their loan approval? What about building inspections? All of these issues can play a major role in determining whether your real estate will close or not in a timely fashion or at all. Most FSBOs generally have problems with sales contracts, and a good knowledge of all contingencies and how they work is suggested and required for any FSBO.

10. The closing. It is always a good idea to make sure the transaction is closed at a local escrow or title insurance company that is certified and insured to participate with a real estate closing. You could also choose a local attorney to close your real estate transaction. But the bottom line is that you should make sure an insured and qualified settlement closing agent is selected.

These are only ten mistakes that many FSBOs make when trying to go down that long road of selling their property on their own; it is not a comprehensive and thorough list of mistakes that could arise, it is a completion of mistakes that occur on a regular basis for many for-sale-by-owners. Naturally for a real estate professional, I encourage all potential home sellers to use the services of a qualified residential real estate agent or an attorney when selling their homes or other properties. However, I understand the need and desire for many people to try to sell their real estate on their own.

How to Save Thousands on Your Next Home Sale

Are you thinking about selling your house or another parcel of real estate that you own? If so, it is important to follow some of these guidelines to help you get the most out of your real estate and possibly save you thousands of dollars in the future. Although this is not a comprehensive list of everything that needs to be followed when deciding to sell your real estate, it is a list of important items that we have noticed at Mayfield Real Estate which can play a big role for most sellers.

- Make sure you list your property with a REALTOR®. As members of the National Association of REALTORS® each member adheres to a strict code of ethics that provide a wide variety of benefits for buyers and sellers. Not all real estate agents are members of the National Association of REALTORS®.
- Have your real estate agent perform a competitive market analysis. Often, real estate agents will not have the information or expertise and know-how to learn what other properties have sold for or what your current competition is. A real estate agent working for you will prepare a competitive CMA so that you can look at what other properties have sold for and what other properties similar to yours are listed for.
- Price your property competitively and correctly from the beginning! Many sellers want to try and get the most out of their property and take the philosophy that they can always adjust the price at a later date. In reality the best and most qualified prospects will come early in the game when the for-sale sign first goes up and your property first hits the local Multiple Listing Service hot sheet. Often, sellers who price their property higher in the beginning and then begin to lower their price over time get less for their property than they would have if it had been priced correctly from the beginning.
- Get a home inspection in advance. Normally a home inspection will not cost you a lot of money and can be a good marketing tool for your agent when selling your property. It is also good because any major issues or problems that might arise can be fixed in advance. Smaller items that can sometimes give the buyer bargaining room to reduce cost can also be prepared or fixed in advance of your marketing efforts and can generally save you hundreds if not thousands of dollars.
- Reduce clutter. It is important to remember that reducing clutter and as much furniture and other items in advance can help in the sale of your property. If you need to store things in boxes or pack things up and move to another location or to another family member or friend's property, the extra room can normally be a benefit.
- Give your home a fresh coat of paint. Generally speaking, a fresh coat of paint and cleaning the carpets is very important in helping you sell your property. Normally painting your home will not cost much and can add a good, fresh appeal to prospective buyers.
- Open the drapes and turn on lights. It is always a good idea to allow as much light into your property as possible. Turning on lights, adding new, stronger light bulbs, and opening blinds and drapes is a big plus for marketing your property.
- Avoid music, and being home when your property is shown. Although many sellers like to be present during the showing of their property, for a real estate agent your absence can help immensely in the marketing of your property. Buyers normally feel *free* to open closets and look at the property without sellers following them around or talking too much about the property. You might also give the wrong information or come off as desperate to sell by being present during the showing.
- Provide copies of receipts on items you have purchased for your agent or repairs you have made over the last couple of years. If you have installed a new roof and you have a copy of how much you spent for the roof, that information can be helpful to

put into a folder or book along with any other major expenses or expenditures you have had. It is also a good idea to have copies of your taxes, the insurance premiums, utility bills, and any other important information, such as surveys or plats that may be available to help your real estate agent during the marketing process.

- Clean the front porch and front lawn of any debris or items that might be a turn off people are driving by to look at your property. Making sure your lawn is mowed and well manicured, along with a cleanly swept front porch without a lot of debris, is very important in the marketing efforts of your property.

- Make your home look like one in a magazine. Having your beds made, clothes picked up off the floor, tables straightened, and rooms fit for a picture in a magazine is important and can be a big hit when buyers tour your property, for a possible home purchase.

- Be open to suggestions from your agent. It is always important to remember that your real estate agent is the professional and has the expertise or know-how in selling your property. Many agents will report back to your listing agent as to what buyers or other agents think about your property or what needs to be fixed or changed. If this is the case, be sure to have an open mind and listen to any suggestions that your agent may have to improve the market ability of your property.

Again, this is not a comprehensive list of what you need to do to sell your property, but incorporating these few suggestions will help immensely in the marketing of your property to get you the most out of your real estate, resulting in and for a happy and successful closing. For more information about any of Mayfield Real Estate listings, visit our Web site at www.Mayfieldre.com; you can also e-mail us if you have other questions at JohnM@MayfieldRe.com

Ten Tips for Selling Your Home Smoothly

1. Make an "I'll Miss List!" There are several items you'll probably miss when you leave your house. These items are normally excellent marketing features to promote to potential buyers. Take time to make note of the things you enjoy and will miss when the sale is completed and you've moved from your house. Items you appreciate are items someone else will enjoy too!

2. Know the facts! Most buyers will have questions about taxes, lot size, utility costs, and other pertinent information about your property. It's always a good idea to know the facts and to have this information available for potential consumers looking at your real estate. Take time to research this information and have it readily available for buyers and/or real estate agents.

3. Recent repairs. Most borrowers need to know about any recent updates, repairs, or additions you've made to your home. For example, a new roof, furnace or central air-conditioning unit and water heater are all important to note. If so, what was the cost, when was it installed, and who did the work are all noteworthy features to have for buyers and agents when selling your property. Any items of repaired or newly added

during your tenure should be listed on a separate sheet if at all possible. It's also a good idea to furnish copies of paid receipts if you choose on the items repaired or installed to validate these costs. Sometimes placing this information in a binder is a good marketing feature to show buyers and agents.

4. Replace light bulbs. Changing light bulbs to a higher wattage can be an aid in brightening rooms and giving a more spacious feel to your home overall. Always check the light fixture and the maximum wattage and do not add bulbs above the recommended usage. You can also add a drop of vanilla extract to bulbs on lamps to aid in providing a fresh smell to rooms if needed.

5. Remove heirlooms or keepsakes. Many times sellers will want to keep certain items that have sentimental value to them such as a light fixture or wall mirror that has been affixed to the real property. If you have an item that you plan to replace, then you should do so prior to any showing. Once buyers visit your property and begin making offers to purchase your property, it's generally hard to negotiate these items off of the offer to purchase.

6. Clean the gutters and add extensions where needed. You never know when your property may be shown, and if it's raining that day, the last thing you want to portray is a house in which the water is gushing over the gutters and downspouts. Making sure the gutters are clean and that extensions move water away from your foundation is always a good idea for continued maintenance of your home, but also for showing buyers your commitment to caring for your home and keeping it in tip-top shape.

7. Hire a building inspector. Let's face it—you want to sell your home. If so, it's probably not a bad idea to have a building inspector look at your home and make a list of repairs or items that need to be fixed prior to marketing your property. After all, many home buyers will have a home inspection too; so this type of preinspection will help fix in advance any potential problems a future inspector might have to correct. Many buyers will also get "cold" feet if the inspector shows too many needed repairs on their report. By fixing these issues in advance you can ward off these potential future problems.

8. Don't appear too anxious! Many sellers will sometimes point out too many facts or features about the home and often sound too anxious to sell quickly. This attitude can hurt you by costing additional thousands of dollars when negotiating with the buyers. You might note that this is one reason many sellers feel the need to hire a real estate agent to help with buyer negotiations.

9. Have your house appraised. It's usually a good idea to hire an independent appraiser when you're selling on your own. This way you'll know and feel certain that you are getting top dollar for your home. According to the NAR Profile of Buyers and Sellers, 2006 edition, most FSBOs could have sold their homes for more money if they had been assisted by a real estate agent.

10. Call me if you have questions. If you do have any questions or concerns that arise in the near future, please don't hesitate to give me a call. Although I am limited on what advice or help I can provide under our state real estate license law and rules and regulations, I will be glad to assist on any questions that are permissible. If you decide to list your home in the future, I would love to help there too—just give me a call!

Summary

As a real estate professional for over 28 years, one of my greatest assets and the biggest aid to my success has been the FSBO. Remind yourself that many real estate agents will contact FSBOs one or two times. However, those who maintain consistency and follow-up on a regular basis, building friendships, will find the FSBO a rewarding and gratifying experience. I encourage you to begin a systematic FSBO action plan and not to give up easily when contacting this type of prospect. Consistency, follow-up, and building friendships are the three main ingredients to employ when contacting FSBOs.

4 Expired Listings

Introduction

The expired listing is an excellent source of business but is seldom worked efficiently and effectively by many real estate professionals. As we've discussed throughout this book, prospecting is a critical element to your success as a real estate agent. Finding your niche and an area of prospecting that you feel comfortable with is important if you want to have a long and prosperous career.

Why work expired listings?

- The expired-listing clients are normally more motivated than when they originally listed their property.
- Expired-listing clients are already familiar with the process of marketing.
- These listings provide an excellent opportunity for you to shine above the competition.
- It is normally easier to obtain a price adjustment from an expired listing client.
- The expired-listing client will generally be easier to negotiate with on submitted offers.
- There's a "fresh" new set of expired-listing prospects everyday through your local Multiple Listing Service (MLS).

The Game Plan

Now that I've demonstrated that the expired listing is a viable and worthwhile lead to pursue as a real estate professional, let's develop the game plan to effectively reach this segment of the market.

First, conform to all local, state, and national "do not call" rules when prospecting this group. To do this you will need to develop a game plan through direct mail or face-to-face meetings. For many real estate agents, face-to-face meetings are not much fun; they can be intimidating. However, you must remember that communicating properly with an expired-listing prospect might be more profitable in person rather than through the US Postal Service.

The Face-to-Face Meeting

If you choose to meet an expired-listing customer face-to-face interview, the meeting should be short and simple; also, have some information to leave behind with the consumer. Remind yourself that the introduction should be something as easy as the following:

Hello Mr. and Mrs. Seller. My name is John Mayfield; I am with Mayfield Real Estate. When I was driving through the area, I noticed that you recently had your house listed with XYZ Realty, and according to our MLS it has recently expired. I won't take up much of your time, but I was curious to know if you had re-listed with XYZ Realty?
[Wait for Response]

If " yes, we've re-listed…"

I am sorry to have bothered you. XYZ is an excellent company and I work with them often on other real estate transactions. I will call them for more details. Thank you for your time, and I hope you have a great day.

If "no, we have not re-listed…"

I won't take up much of your time, but I was in your neighborhood and wanted to drop off some information for you. Are you still interested in selling your property?

If "no…"

I understand, and again, I hate to bother you, but I would love to give you some free *information about myself and my company, and if you decide to market your property in the future please keep me in mind.*

If "yes…"

Again, I don't want to take up your time right now since I dropped by unexpectedly, but I would love to give you some information about myself and my company, and if I could stop by at a later time, I would love to visit with you and share some of the marketing ideas and strategies that have helped me sell properties similar to your house. Could I have your permission to call in the next day or two to set up a visit with you to discuss your real estate needs?

As shown, the face-to-face interview needs to be short, simple, and to the point. Always find out if the prospect has a written agency agreement with someone else prior to moving forward with your marketing endeavors. If the prospect does not have a written agency agreement, then it's okay to proceed with providing information and attempting to set up an appointment at a later date. It's also a good idea to check your local MLS prior to visiting the expired listing to make certain that no one else has listed the property for sale. If you see another real estate company's sign in front of the property, do not call on the expired listing. Always check the MLS immediately before initiating a face-to-face interview with an expired-listing consumer!

Try to have information readily available for the consumer if they're not in an agency relationship. Customizing materials for the prospective customer/client is good to do in advance. We'll explore this in more detail later in the chapter.

Be sure to check local and state real estate commission rules and regulations prior to prospecting expired listings to make certain that you are within the law.

The Packet

Now that you've conducted the face-to-face interview with the expired-listing customer, and there is a possibility of listing the property since there is no agency relationship with another company, it's time to explore the type of information you should have for your potential client.

As in the chapter on for-sale-by-owners and many of the other handouts provided in this manual, information about yourself and your company needs to be included with this presentation. However, it's always good to customize your material for the consumer at hand. Let's explore some of the issues the expired-listing consumer will be familiar with from being listed with another agent and not having their home sell.

- **Lack of Communication:** Research tells us that most real estate professionals fail to communicate with their clients on a regular basis. With that in mind, a major portion of your presentation needs to demonstrate your ability to "stay in touch" with your clients! Having information in your packet that discusses your commitment to communication and prompt follow-up feedback will be a good marketing point to cover in your expired-listing materials. The following page shows a sample handout that addresses this point.

I'll stay in touch

We're Not #1, You Are!

John Mayfield GRI, CRB, ABR
509 East Main St.
Park Hills, MO 63601

I promise:

- To keep you informed of all information about the sale of your home in a timely manner
- To provide regular updates after all showings
- To provide you with regular updates regarding the local housing market, i.e., sales, new listings, and more
- To negotiate any and all offers on your behalf
- To market and advertise your property aggressively to achieve a fast and prompt sale
- To send you copies of all advertisements and marketing ideas generated
- To make the sale of your property as hassle *free* as possible
- To make you a client for life!

Office: 573-756-0077
Fax: 573-756-1336
Cell: 573-760-4220
E-mail:
John@RealEstateTechGuy.com
Web site:
www.RealEstateTechGuy.com

- **Discouragement of Issues:** This includes having no lookers or having many lookers but no offers. One possible means to combat both of these issues is through the use of an updated competitive market analysis. The following two postcards show examples of how both of these topics could be addressed.

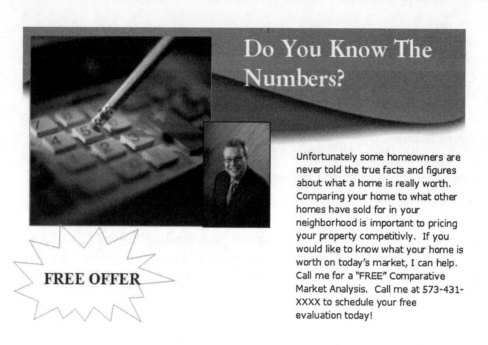

Do You Know The Numbers?

Unfortunately some homeowners are never told the true facts and figures about what a home is really worth. Comparing your home to what other homes have sold for in your neighborhood is important to pricing your property competitivly. If you would like to know what your home is worth on today's market, I can help. Call me for a "FREE" Comparative Market Analysis. Call me at 573-431-XXXX to schedule your free evaluation today!

FREE OFFER

Wondering Why?

Wondering why your home did not sell? Unfortunately there could be many reasons and factors on why your home is still unsold. The good news is, I can help evaluate the situation and provide new insights and ideas on what the problem or problems may be. Call me, John Mayfield for a "FREE" no obligation price evaluation on what your home is worth on today's market. Call John Mayfield at 573-431-XXXX today!

Check out my "FREE" Reports at
www.RealEstateTechGuy.com

What's Your Commitment to Marketing?

If this is an area that you do not (or cannot) financially live up to, hopefully your company can assist with this part of your game plan. A proposed marketing plan should be included in your leave-behind presentation. Other topics and ideas to be included are:

- Sample statistics
- Newsletter
- Copy of Web site
- Photos or virtual tours
- Testimonial letters
- Agent resume
- Awards and other designations
- List of satisfied clients and customers they can call
- Thank you letter

If you plan to use a leave-behind marketing presentation, be aware that it could end up in the hands of a competitor. For this reason, many real estate professionals are reluctant to leave information behind. Weigh the pros and cons before leaving a marketing presentation in the hands of a consumer.

Contacting the Expired Listing through Direct Mail

With many real estate professionals, using the face-to-face meeting is not a popular method. It's hard to imagine why real estate agents dislike the in-person interview, but unfortunately there is some sort of fear that makes most people dislike an informal first-time meeting with strangers. If that's an issue, using the direct mail approach might be more to your liking. This section will provide you with possible ideas to incorporate in a direct mail approach. Remember that if you plan to effectively win the expired-listings businesses, then you need to contact the expired-listing customer on a regular basis!

Your direct mail plan needs to be consistent to be effective, too! To help you accomplish this action plan, a list of letters and postcard ideas are included for your use. Many of the letters and postcards utilize value-added opportunities through the use of *"free"* reports. You can also add digital photos of the prospective property to the expired-listing letter/flyer. The following example illustrates an expired-listing flyer with photos of the expired listing incorporated within the marketing piece.

Did You Know?

Your home is no longer for sale in our MLS...

John Mayfield GRI, CRB, ABR
509 East Main St.
Park Hills, MO 63601

If you're still considering selling your property, I would love to visit with you about a marketing campaign I designed for expired listings. After you see this presentation and marketing campaign, I feel confident and know you'll agree that it will be beneficial to you. Sometimes a change of direction and a fresh breath of air are just what expired listings need to sell quickly.

I have enclosed a report entitled *"5 Important Marketing Strategies That I'll Employ for You."* These are just a few of the many marketing ideas I implement for all of my listing clients. It's also available from my Web site at *[agent's Web site]*. You can reach me at 431-3667 to arrange an appointment to hear more about my marketing campaign.

As always, thank you for your time, and I do hope to hear from you soon.

Office: 573-756-0077
Fax: 573-756-1336
Cell: 573-760-4220
E-mail:
John@RealEstateTechGuy.com
Web site:
www.RealEstateTechGuy.com

Working expired listings can be a rewarding prospecting tool if done correctly. First, it's important to remember that the expired-listing prospect is discouraged and may have a bad impression of the real estate professional. Of course, this depends on the type of communication and marketing efforts delivered to them from their previous real estate agent. Therefore, remind yourself when prospecting the expired-listing customer that it may take time and consistency to be effective. Generally, most prospects are bombarded by many agents attempting to get their business in the first week or two after their listing expires. However, most of these attempts by other real estate agents will be short-lived and fail to deliver a follow-up program that effectively builds a relationship and gains the prospect's trust. Therefore, only those real estate agents who maintain a consistent and continuous follow-up program (without badgering or bugging the prospect) will have the best opportunity to get the expired-listing business. The expired-listing prospect may choose to take their house off the market temporarily, but as a general rule, once a month or two has passed, the need or desire to sell and relocate as originally planned becomes prominent again. Think about your own life for a moment. Have you ever wanted to trade automobiles but gave up because you could not find the right car or were offered a price well below what you wanted? How many times did you try to sell your car on your own only to find yourself making the switch 30 or 60 days later? The same principle applies to expired-listing customers who say they're taking their house off the market for a while. The need to sell will resurface in the near future. For this simple reason it's important to have a good follow-up program with the expired-listing prospect.

Keep in mind the attitude the expired-listing prospect can have about the real estate industry. The following points may help shed some light on this type of potential client and on how to overcome various objections they might have.

Discouraged from lack of communication from the previous listing agent
Property was not shown during entire listing period
Lack of advertising or marketing materials about their property
Many lookers but no offers or feedback
No direction or help from previous listing agent

As you can see, the expired-listing prospect has two major problems with re-listing with another agent. First, there may have been a lack of communication between the agent/agency and themselves. Second, the expired-listing prospect is discouraged because of too many showings and no contracts or no showings at all during the listing period. Generally the expired-listing customer faces one major problem in getting their home sold—the price! As one motivational speaker commented at a real estate function, a price is never too high for a property. There is someone out there in the community who will pay the price you have on your property. They may have been born today, but yes, someone out there will have pay the asking price you have on your property! Pricing plays an integral role in selling real estate. Even a home on a busy street, if it's priced right, will have someone who will invest in it.

Your job is to help explain the price to the expired-listing prospect. For this reason, most of the materials you produce should address your ability to both communicate more effectively than the competitors and help the prospect understand how their real estate should be priced. Being able to handle these two objections is essential for gaining the trust of the expired-listing prospect and his or her business.

The following pages detail a few sample letters you might consider using when prospecting for expired listings.

509 East Main St.
Park Hills, MO 63601
Office: 573-756-0077
Cell: 573-760-4220 Fax: 573-756-1336
Email: John@RealEstateTechGuy.com
Website: www.RealEstateTechGuy.com

We're Not #1, You Are!

[Date]

«Address Block»

«Greeting Line»

Hello, my name is *[agent's name]*, and I am with *[agency name]*. Today, while doing my daily market research through our local Multiple Listing Service, I noticed that your home is no longer listed for sale. I have an excellent track record *[If you're new to the business, be sure and emphasis your company here.]* for helping customers whose properties could not sell with other firms. I have a *free* report, *"5 Reasons Why Your Home Probably Didn't Sell,"* that I would love to share with you. You can visit my Web site at *[agent's Web address]* and download it, or, if you do not have access to the Internet, I would be happy to mail you this *free* report. You can call me at *[agent's phone number]*.

I appreciate your time, and I would love to visit with you about your real estate needs at your earliest convenience.

Sincerely,

[Agent's Name]
[Agent's Title]

509 East Main St.
Park Hills, MO 63601
Office: 573-756-0077
Cell: 573-760-4220 Fax: 573-756-1336
Email: John@RealEstateTechGuy.com
Website: www.RealEstateTechGuy.com

We're Not #1, You Are!

[Date]

«Address Block»

«Greeting Line»

Hi, my name is *[agent's name]*, and I am with *[agency name]*. Today, while doing my daily market research through our local Multiple Listing Service, I noticed that your home is no longer listed for sale or accessible through our local database. If you have already re-listed your home, please disregard this letter, but if you would like a *free* property diagnosis why your property failed to sell, I would be happy to do this for you. My analysis does not take too long and will provide you with concrete reasons why your home failed to sell. If this is something you would be interested in, please feel *free* to call me at *[agent's phone number]* and I will be glad to schedule an appointment with you.

You can also visit my Web site at *[agent's Web address]* to get more information useful for buyers and sellers.

I do appreciate your time, and I would love the opportunity to visit with you regarding your real estate needs. I hope to hear from you soon.

Sincerely,

[Agent's Name]
[Agent's Title]

509 East Main St.
Park Hills, MO 63601
Office: 573-756-0077
Cell: 573-760-4220 Fax: 573-756-1336
Email: John@RealEstateTechGuy.com
Website: www.RealEstateTechGuy.com

We're Not #1, You Are!

[Date]

«Address Block»

«Greeting Line»

I know you are probably being bombarded by those who have noticed your property is no longer for sale in our local Multiple Listing Service. Naturally, I am one of many real estate professionals who feel certain I can solve your problem and get your home sold in a reasonable amount of time, virtually hassle *free*, and for the best possible sales price. First of all, I want you to know that, as a real estate professional, I cannot make any guarantees or promises in selling your property; however, I can promise exceptional customer service and communication that is unmatched by anyone else in our marketplace. My goal is to make the selling and buying of real estate a pleasant experience appreciated by all of my customers. The end result is hopefully a successful transaction.

If you have any questions, please feel *free* to call me anytime. I have enclosed a "FREE" report entitled *"5 Reasons Why Your Home Probably Didn't Sell"* that I would love to share with you. You can also visit my Web site at *[agent's Web address]* and download this report for *free*. If you do not have access to the Internet, I would be happy to mail this "FREE" report to you. You can call me at *[agent's phone number]*.

I appreciate your time, and I would love to visit with you about your real estate needs at your earliest convenience.

Sincerely,

[Agent's Name]
[Agent's Title]

509 East Main St.
Park Hills, MO 63601
Office: 573-756-0077
Cell: 573-760-4220 Fax: 573-756-1336
Email: John@RealEstateTechGuy.com
Website: www.RealEstateTechGuy.com

We're Not #1, You Are!

[Date]

«Address Block»

«Greeting Line»

Did you know?

Did you know your home is no longer for sale in our local Multiple Listing Service computer database? Since your listing expired, your home is no longer available to potential buyers and real estate agents through our Multiple Listing Service. If you're still considering selling your property, I would love to visit with you about the marketing campaign I have designed for expired listings. I feel confident that you'll agree, after seeing this presentation and marketing campaign, that it would be beneficial for you. Sometimes a change of direction and a fresh breath of air is all an expired listing needs to sell quickly.

I have enclosed a report entitled *"5 Important Marketing Strategies That I'll Employ for You."* These are just a few of the many marketing ideas I have implemented for all of my listing clients. It's also available from my Web site at *[agent's Web address]*. You can reach me at *[agent's phone number]* to arrange an appointment to hear more about my marketing campaign.

As always, thank you for your time, and I do hope to hear from you soon.

Sincerely,

[Agent's Name]
[Agent's Title]

509 East Main St.
Park Hills, MO 63601
Office: 573-756-0077
Cell: 573-760-4220 Fax: 573-756-1336
Email: John@RealEstateTechGuy.com
Website: www.RealEstateTechGuy.com

We're Not #1, You Are!

[Date]

«Address Block»

«Greeting Line»

Selling Your Home Doesn't Have To Be That Difficult

If you've been frustrated or discouraged by the process of trying to sell your home, don't get too discouraged—I have several marketing techniques that I think can help you sell your property quickly. For a "FREE", no-pressure and no-obligation consultation and appointment to hear more about these marketing ideas, call me at *[agent's phone number]*.

Feel *free* to check out my Web site at *[agent's Web address]* for some of the marketing techniques I'm employing for my clients.

Thank you for your time, and I hope to hear from you soon.

Sincerely,

[Agent's Name]
[Agent's Title]

509 East Main St.
Park Hills, MO 63601
Office: 573-756-0077
Cell: 573-760-4220 Fax: 573-756-1336
Email: John@RealEstateTechGuy.com
Website: www.RealEstateTechGuy.com

We're Not #1, You Are!

[Date]

«Address Block»

«Greeting Line»

Don't Just Take My Word on It

I know many times real estate agents talk a big game, but when it comes to delivering results, it can sometimes be a different scenario. Rather than explaining a little bit about my customer service in this letter, I thought it would be good to enclose some brief testimonies from my satisfied customers and clients. As you will see from these letters, my service and commitment to you go beyond the call of duty.

I do hope that you will give me an opportunity to visit with you about your real estate needs. You can reach me at *[agent's phone number]*. Thank you for your time, and I do hope to hear from you soon.

Sincerely,

[Agent's Name]
[Agent's Title]

Expired-Listing Kit

If you're considering building an "expired-listing" kit, the following list gives some idea of what you might consider including:

> Introduction letter
> Recap of local market
> *Free* report
> Sample flyer
> Copy of a proposed marketing plan
> Testimonial letters
> Agent resume
> Company resume
> Now that your home is no longer listed, what does that mean?
> Ten tips for a successful negotiation
> Easy exit agreement
> Agent comparison chart or company comparison chart

Ten Reasons Why Your Home Probably Didn't Sell

This report I have developed outlines ten reasons a home may not have sold while listed with another real estate company. While these may not portray the exact facts of your case, these scenarios do depict situations that hinder the selling of many listed homes. Please note that these assertions are merely this agent's conclusions and are not meant to suggest wrong doings on the part of any real estate company or agent.

1. **Your Property Was Priced Too High!** Like it or not, price is generally the main culprit when it comes to homes not selling. Yes, the property might be in a poor location or there may be other negative factors, but the bottom line is that somewhere out there, there is a buyer willing to purchase the real estate at "some" price. If the price is attractive enough, there is always a willing buyer. Making certain your real estate is priced at market value is important if you're serious about selling.

2. **Your property Was Not in the MLS.** If your agent did not belong to the Multiple Listing Service, then your home may not have been exposed to the necessary number of agents. It's imperative that your property be in the correct position in the local MLS to gain maximum exposure to agents in your area.

3. **Lack of Staging.** Did your real estate agent help stage the home? If not, this could be contributing to the lack of buyers for your property. (Remember that you can do all the staging in the world, but if your real estate is priced too high, the staging will not work). One ways to determine if a lack of staging is a negative factor is by comparing the ratio of showings to offers. If you've experienced a lot of showings but few or no offers, then staging might help.

4. **Photos.** The purpose of this report is to not disparage or take advantage of the competition; it is to help draw realistic conclusions by asking questions about why your property did not sell. Many times as a real estate professional I have noticed properties listed that had few, if any, photos or virtual tours added to the local MLS or company Web site. I cannot commit on this fact or issue. This may or may not be the case with your property, but it is an area you should question to determine whether or not it can be improved upon.

5. **Lack of Facts.** Sometimes a commonly overlooked aspect of marketing a home involves a lack of information. Did your agent have the needed facts to convey to buyers and other agents any updates and/or additions to your property? These facts can be a good marketing tool to use with potential buyers to show them what improvements and upgrades have been made to your property. This information is very helpful to both agents and buyers during property showings.

6. **Lack of Open Houses.** Many agents do not like to hold open houses for the public or other real estate agents. I believe it is important to expose as many people as possible (other agents) to the properties I have for sale. Open houses are an excellent way to get people inside your dwelling and interested in the property! The more marketing programs, the better for everyone involved, and one of my most popular marketing tools is the open house.

7. **Working with the Neighbors.** Who better to sell your home than your neighbors? That's not to say your neighbors will be glad to see you leave, only that they will be concerned about who might move in. Many times the neighbors in your area would love to help find the right family, one that they are acquainted with and know on a personal level. It feels good having friends living close by, and usually if your neighbors can help sell your property to people they know, they will! This is generally a winning proposition for everyone involved. As a real estate professional, if I'm chosen to work for you, I promise to work closely with your neighbors to insure they have the needed information to share with any friends or acquaintances who might be interested in your home.

8. **No Internet Presence.** Unfortunately, many real estate agents still do not have their own Web sites. Many buyers consult the World Wide Web for information about homes for sale. If your property was not properly positioned on the Web for these new tech-savvy buyers, then you've missed a golden opportunity for potential buyers. I will make sure your property is placed on our Web site and given full exposure to Internet buyers shopping for a home in our marketplace.

9. **Communication.** One of the main goals and functions of a property lister is making certain the listing is conveyed to the other real estate agents in a community. Marketing flyers and property data sheets with detailed information in flyer boxes, along with other important features about your home, need to be readily available for the buying public. Perhaps your property needed more of a push with other agents in the area. One of my main functions is keeping properties in the forefront of other real estate agents minds. My philosophy is that

the agents in our marketplace may have a buyer on any given day. Making sure they are exposed to your listing is essential to helping speed up the sale of your property. After all, most homes are sold by someone other than the listing agent; therefore, seeing that your property details are know by other top agents in our board is essential!

10. **Some Properties Just Don't Sell!** Unfortunately, there are times when the services of even the best agent in an area can't sell your house. As noted earlier, there are many great real estate agents in a given community and many work very hard at what they do. Sadly, not all properties sell, nor can your property be shown in every situation. It's never a good idea for an agent to make a seller "think" he or she has prospects when they don't.

Don't be discouraged if your house didn't sell on the first go-around. Make sure your property is priced correctly, follow the suggestions within these tips, and have a positive outlook; I'm certain your real estate will sell soon.

Often during my real estate career I've taken houses listed unsuccessfully by other agents and sold them quickly. Other agents have done likewise with some of my unsuccessful listings. I don't have all of the reasons or facts why this happens; I can only say that a fresh new sign, a new marketing plan, and a change can often be a good thing for everyone involved.

TEN THINGS TO CONSIDER BEFORE RE-LISTING YOUR HOME FOR SALE

1. Have your agent (or new agent) do an updated competitive market analysis on the current market conditions.
2. Consider having a home-staging company review your property and consult with you on what improvements might be done.
3. Consider removing excess furniture from smaller rooms.
4. Find out what type of feedback your previous agent received from showings.
5. Drive by other properties for sale in your neighborhood and compare their price to yours to see if your home is listed higher than those in your marketplace.
6. Check if walls, trim, or doors need painting.
7. Consider having the carpets cleaned by a professional company.
8. Prepare a home marketing book with detailed information about your property.
9. Have your new real estate agent provide you with a detailed marketing plan for selling your property.
10. Remember that in some slower markets, properties take time to sell. If you're in a hurry, you may have to adjust your price in order to stand out among your competitors.

5 Sphere of Influence

Contacting your sphere of influence (SOI), sometimes referred to as center of influence (COI), is an important and integral part of the real estate professional's success. For the purposes of this manual, we will refer to this group as "sphere of influence," or SOI.

According to the National Association of REALTORS® 2006 Profile of Home Buyers and Sellers, 40% of all buyers found their agent through referral by a friend, neighbor, and/or relative. Of the first-time buyers, 49% attested to this fact, while 35% of repeat buyers found their agents through the same referral method. As you can see, a large number of buyers find real estate agents through recommendations from friends, family members, or neighbors. I hope that reading this initial section and verifying these statistics will encourage and persuade you to develop a group of contacts you know well and communicate with on a regular basis to be part of your SOI.

Your SOI should be a group of people who recommend you for real estate services when they come upon such opportunities in their daily lives. think of real estate. It's important that you're contacting your SOI not just for their business, but also to encourage them to suggest your real estate services to others. You're basically asking your SOI to scout opportunities for you to list and sell real estate. Therefore, most of the marketing pieces you construct for your SOI need to emphasise your expertise in and knowledge of the real estate field and your marketplace. Your postcards, flyers, and letters should present a softer sell to recipients and encourage them to suggest you to friends, coworkers, and family members. Information about the marketplace, about you, and about what you're accomplishing as a real estate professional is good to use. Try not to toot your horn too loud; rather, focus on the "informational" aspect of your real estate career. As a real estate professional, you can provide to your SOI reports about the market area, tips and fact sheets on properties to avoid, and information on homes you've sold. As with all areas of prospecting, consistency is essential for this type of lead generation to work.

Some agents use an 8 x 8 or 6 x 6 program of contact. The author encourages a 30/15 rule to contact your SOI for gaining maximum exposure and success. Both of these methods will be discussed later in this chapter. Regardless of which method you implement, it is important to prospect your SOI on a regular and continuous basis so that, over time, they always remember you as the expert in the real estate business. You need to train your SOI to help you in your marketplace and to be on the lookout for new leads you can work. When you can effectively implement a powerful SOI program on a consistent basis, you will see your real estate career improve by leaps and bounds!

Here's an example of how you might consider contacting your SOI using the 30/15 rule over a calendar year. The 30/15 rule utilizes your SOI but breaks the list into two groups: an A Group and a B Group. Your A Group (20% of the people whom you feel will send you regular leads) needs a "touch" or contact at least 30 times a year. The B Group (80% of the people who will send leads, though not as many as your A Group) need a "touch" 15 times a year. This theory relies on the 80/20 principle, where 20% of the people are doing the bulk of the work— they send you the most leads. The following pages outline a possible way you might consider appling the 30/15 rule to contact your SOI.

The 30/15 Rule

Touches a Year

Write down your total number of contacts with your sphere of influence list:

1. Total contacts =

2. Total contacts × 0.80 =

3. *Subtract* that number (answer 2) from your total contacts (answer 1).

Your answer in line 3 represents 20% of the contacts in your sphere of influence.

Note that to effectively implement the 30/15 rule, you must identify the 80% of your audience who will not send referrals to you on a "regular" basis. Please understand that this *does not* mean you will never receive referrals from these people, only that they will not contribute leads to you continuously. This list of names will need a "touch," but not as often as your 20% list requires!

For the 30/15 rule to be effective, you need to do the following:

- Contact 80% of your SOI 15+ times a year.
- Contact 20% of your SOI 30+ times a year.

A "touch" is _____ form of _____ to your contact!
Here are a few ideas to help implement the 30/15 rule.

15 Touches for your 80% Group" (B Group)

One mailing per month = a *touch!*
One phone call every four months = a *touch!*
Your 80% group now receives a minimum of 15 touches per year from you!

30 Touches for your 20% Group (A Group)

One mailing per month = a *touch!*
One birthday card sent per contact per year in your 20% list = a *touch!*
One phone call per contact per month in your 20% list = a *touch!*
One basket of cookies delivered to your 20% list per year = a *touch!*
One Spring theme card mailed to your 20% list per year = a *touch!*
One 4th of July card mailed to your 20% list per year = a *touch!*
One Thanksgiving card mailed to your 20% list per year = a *touch!*
One Christmas or Hanukkah card mailed to your 20% list per year = a *touch!*
    Additional "touches" that could count:

- Movie or bowling night
- Customer appreciation picnic or event
- After-the-sale open house for buyers
- Letters as included at the end of chapter

Another popular means of contacting your SOI is through a method sometimes referred to as "Power of 8." Through this procedure you will contact your SOI eight times over an 8 week period. Most agents use the same postcard for contacting their SOI during this 8 week period. Some agents will vary the look of the postcard; however, the author has heard of better results from the use of unaltered postcards. The following example shows a sample postcard you might use for your "Power of 8" direct mail campaign.

509 East Main St.
Park Hills, MO 63601

mayfield

PRSRT STD
U.S. POSTAGE PAID
CITY, STATE
YOUR PERMIT NO.

Office: 573-756-0077
Fax: 573-756-1336
Cell: 573-760-4220
Email: John@RealEstateTechGuy.com
Website: www.RealEstateTechGuy.com

John Mayfield GRI, CRB, ABR

«FirstName» «LastName»
«Address1» «Address2»
«City» «State» «PostalCode»

Type Text Here

Now Accepting New Clients

Sold!

Sold!

If you're in the market to buy or sell, call me today! Call John at 431-3667!

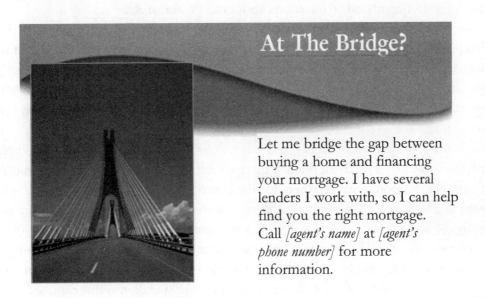

At The Bridge?

Let me bridge the gap between buying a home and financing your mortgage. I have several lenders I work with, so I can help find you the right mortgage. Call *[agent's name]* at *[agent's phone number]* for more information.

Note, this ad copy taken from 5-Minutes to a Great Real Estate Ad, Thomson/Learning

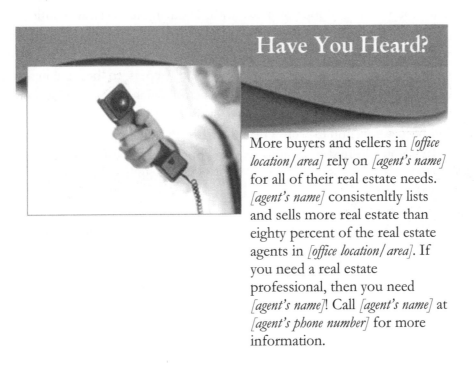

Have You Heard?

More buyers and sellers in *[office location/area]* rely on *[agent's name]* for all of their real estate needs. *[agent's name]* consistenltly lists and sells more real estate than eighty percent of the real estate agents in *[office location/area]*. If you need a real estate professional, then you need *[agent's name]*! Call *[agent's name]* at *[agent's phone number]* for more information.

Photos in post card examples are from Digital Juice. These graphics and photo packages can be purchased separately from www.DigitalJuice.com.

Here are a few frequently asked questions about the Power of 8:

What makes the "Power of 8" so successful? The author believes it's the repetition of the message that helps drive the following point home: when you think of real estate, think of me.

Is it okay to alter the program? No. It's best to follow the rules, sending one postcard per week to the same audience with the same message for a total of 8 weeks. If someone calls or writes requesting removal from the marketing campaign, then be sure them from your mailing list.

Who are the best prospects to send the Power of 8 postcards to? Normally your SOI is a good place to start with the Power of 8 method, but any group, such as a neighborhood, subdivision, or apartment complex, is good target prospect for the Power of 8.

Will people get mad at receiving so many postcards from me over such a short period of time? Any good sales professional will attest that to be effective you must prospect. If you don't ask for the business, someone else will! If a prospect does get frustrated with your Power of 8 program and asks to be removed, simply apologize for the inconvenience and remove them from your list. I believe you'll find only a small percentage of contacts fall into this category.

Who Goes on Your SOI List?

A good place to generate your SOI list is to pretend you or one of your children is getting married. Whom will you invite to the wedding? Normally these friends and family members are an excellent group to begin your SOI list with. From there you can continue to add names as you think of them, and be sure to include any new clients you business with as a real estate agent. Keep a list in your car or briefcase so you can add names on the spot.

Once you have your SOI list complete, your next step is to begin contacting and communicating with your group on a regular basis. The following pages provide some letters and postcard campaigns you might consider using. You can find the letters on the enclosed CD-ROM. The postcard examples were created with HP Real Estate Marketing Assistant Software (REMA). You can find more information about REMA software on the enclosed CD-ROM.

> Note: for additional letters, please check out 5 Minutes to a Great Real Estate Letter, published by Thomson Learning.

509 East Main St.
Park Hills, MO 63601
Office: 573-756-0077
Cell: 573-760-4220 Fax: 573-756-1336
Email: John@RealEstateTechGuy.com
Website: www.RealEstateTechGuy.com

We're Not #1, You Are!

[Date]

«Address Block»

«Greeting Line»

I wanted to let you know that I am now affiliated with *[company name]* as a real estate professional. *[Company name]* has been in business for *[x number of]* years and has a long and successful track record with their customers and clients. I chose *[company name]* because of their company philosophy, education and training, and commitment to excellence in customer service. If you or someone you know has any real estate needs, please keep me in mind. I have enclosed several business cards for you to pass along to anyone you know who is in the market to buy or sell real estate.

As always, thank you for your time and friendship, and I hope to hear from you soon.

Sincerely,

[Agent's Name]
[Agent's Title]

509 East Main St.
Park Hills, MO 63601
Office: 573-756-0077
Cell: 573-760-4220 Fax: 573-756-1336
Email: John@RealEstateTechGuy.com
Website: www.RealEstateTechGuy.com

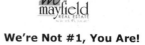

We're Not #1, You Are!

[Date]

«Address Block»

«Greeting Line»

Purchasing a home is one of the biggest decisions a person makes in his or her lifetime. Having someone they can trust to clearly explain the home-buying and home-selling process is important for a smooth transaction. As a friend of yours, I want you to keep me in mind for people you know who may be considering buying or selling real estate. I have enclosed several business cards for you to distribute to those you know or come into contact with who may need my services.

As always, I appreciate your friendship and your willingness to help me succeed with my real estate career. Thanks so much, and I hope it's a great week for you!

Sincerely,

[Agent's Name]
[Agent's Title]

509 East Main St.
Park Hills, MO 63601
Office: 573-756-0077
Cell: 573-760-4220 Fax: 573-756-1336
Email: John@RealEstateTechGuy.com
Website: www.RealEstateTechGuy.com

We're Not #1, You Are!

[Date]

«*Address Block*»

«*Greeting Line*»

According to the National Association of REALTORS®, *[x]* percent of buyers who purchased a home in 2006 found their real estate agent through a recommendation from a friend or family member. That's an amazing statistic and makes me hope friends like you think of me when they come into contact with people who need to buy or sell a home. If you know of a friend who may be considering buying or selling real estate, please pass along one of my business cards to them. Your referral is valued and appreciated.

As always, thank you for your friendship, time, and, most of all, for thinking of me when you know of someone who is considering buying or selling real estate.

Sincerely,

[Agent's Name]
[Agent's Title]

509 East Main St.
Park Hills, MO 63601
Office: 573-756-0077
Cell: 573-760-4220 Fax: 573-756-1336
Email: John@RealEstateTechGuy.com
Website: www.RealEstateTechGuy.com

We're Not #1, You Are!

[Date]

«Address Block»

«Greeting Line»

By now you are probably aware that I am selling real estate for *[company name]*. After completing the necessary educational requirements and passing the certification exams for our state, I am now licensed and ready to serve you with any of your real estate needs. You might wonder what makes me unique or special enough to receive your business or recommendations to friends and family when there are so many people who have real estate licenses. Well, I have been a lifelong resident of *[area name]*, and I have always enjoyed working with and helping people. Several close friends encouraged me to get my real estate license because they thought this business would be a perfect fit for me. And I must admit: I am enjoying the real estate business!

Please feel *free* to call or drop me an e-mail should you ever need any assistance with your real estate needs. You can reach me at *[agent's phone number]* or e-mail me at *[agent's e-mail address]*. I hope I can count on you to recommend me to any friends or family members of yours who are considering purchasing or selling real estate. I promise they will have my full attention and the best service possible.

Sincerely,

[Agent's Name]
[Agent's Title]

509 East Main St.
Park Hills, MO 63601
Office: 573-756-0077
Cell: 573-760-4220 Fax: 573-756-1336
Email: John@RealEstateTechGuy.com
Website: www.RealEstateTechGuy.com

We're Not #1, You Are!

[Date]

«Address Block»

«Greeting Line»

Wow, what a neat career path I have chosen! It has been a little over a month since the last time I wrote, and I wanted to send another note to update you on how things are going with my real estate career. I have been very busy with new marketing ideas and learning all of the necessary information to move forward in the real estate profession— familiarizing myself with the current contract forms, agency disclosures, our computerized Multiple Listing Service, and much more. It is a job that requires a lot of preparation and hard work. But, I am enjoying every minute of it!

I have enclosed a *free* report entitled *"15 Reasons to Make Sure You Choose the Right Real Estate Professional."* I think you will agree after reading these suggestions and guidelines that recommending the right real estate professional is an important commitment on your part. I hope you enjoy the *free* report, and, most of all, I hope you will remember me should you come across a friend or acquaintance who might need real estate services. Whether buying or selling, I am here to help you or any referral you may send my way.

I want to personally thank you in advance for supporting my business, and I look forward to receiving a referral from you soon. Thanks again, and I hope you have a great day!

Sincerely,

[Agent's Name]
[Agent's Title]

509 East Main St.
Park Hills, MO 63601
Office: 573-756-0077
Cell: 573-760-4220 Fax: 573-756-1336
Email: John@RealEstateTechGuy.com
Website: www.RealEstateTechGuy.com

We're Not #1, You Are!

[Date]

«Address Block»

«Greeting Line»

Did you know the average sale price for *[area]* is *[average sale price]*? That's right: according to our latest Multiple Listing Service statistics, the average sale price for a single family home in *[area]* is *[price]*. In addition to these findings, I have noted that it takes approximately *[number of average days on market]* days to sell a single family home in our community. I have enclosed a detailed report of average sale prices and days spent on market for several types of properties in various areas of our community. I think this information may be of use to you for future reference should you, a family member, or a friend consider purchasing a home.

I hope all is well with you and your family, I appreciate your time, and I hope that I can be of service to you with your real estate needs in the near future. Remember, if you know of anyone who may be interested in buying or selling a home, I would love to help them. Please pass along one of my business cards. I have enclosed several for you to hand out should a possible referral arise.

Thanks again for your support with my real estate career, and I hope to hear from you soon.

Sincerely,

[Agent's Name]
[Agent's Title]

Introductory letter for an experienced agent

509 East Main St.
Park Hills, MO 63601
Office: 573-756-0077
Cell: 573-760-4220 Fax: 573-756-1336
Email: John@RealEstateTechGuy.com
Website: www.RealEstateTechGuy.com

We're Not #1, You Are!

[Date]

«*Address Block*»

«*Greeting Line*»

It is hard to believe that this is my *[number of years]* in real estate. Wow, I guess time goes by fast when you are having fun! One of my goals throughout my real estate tenure has been to develop a consistent method of communication with my friends and past clients. Unfortunately, sometimes we can have good intentions but not follow through with our goals. This letter is a way for me to begin that plan of action that I've wanted to do for so long. Think of it is an introductory letter to let you know I've will be mailing on a regular basis information about your local real estate market and other news I feel will benefit you as a possible home buyer or seller.

I know that many people have supported my real estate career through various ways such as buying, selling, and/or recommending my services to friends and family. For this I want to say thank you and that I value your support.

I hope all goes well with you and you family, and I appreciate your time so much. I look forward to visiting with you in the future, and please do not hesitate to call if you need any help or advice with any real estate needs. I would also appreciate any referrals interested in buying or selling real estate—being a commission-based-only real estate professional, referrals are the lifeblood of my business.

Sincerely,

[Agent's Name]
[Agent's Title]

Year-at-a-Glance for Contacting Your SOI

Use the following table to organize how and when to contact your SOI during the year. There is a sample copy of it on the enclosed CD-ROM for you to print out and use in your daily business.

SOI Annual Planning Guide

Month	Idea	Method of Contact	Group to Contact
January	Power of 8	Direct mail	All
February	Power of 8 continued	Direct mail	All
March	Personal call	Phone call	All
April	Quarterly Sales report	Direct mail	All
May	Tomato plants	Personal visit	A Group
June	Summer city or area events flyer	Direct mail	All
July	Personal call	Phone call	A Group
August	School calendar for days off	Direct mail	All
September	Postcard	Direct mail	All
October	Quarterly sales report	Direct mail	All
November	SOI letter	Direct mail	All
December	Holiday greetings	Direct mail	All

Please keep in mind that you can customize year-at-a-glance to your liking. For some real estate agents, a personal visit or phone call might be more appropriate, while others may want to concentrate on direct mail to reach their SOI. The important point is to set up a plan in advance and stick to it! Once you've developed your plan, transfer tasks to your monthly calendar for implementation during the year.

Scripts and Dialogs to Consider with Your SOI

Since you have decided to gear up your prospecting and marketing efforts with your SOI group, you might encounter some of the following questions. It's a good idea to ask yourself these questions and begin formulating responses.

Just curious: Why are you sending me all of the real estate information now?
Tell me something about your real estate company.

It seems like there are a lot of people selling real estate these days.

How are you doing with your real estate career?

What are most homes selling for in our neighborhood?

What are homes selling for on average in our city?

Is now a good time to buy or sell a home?

Why did you send me all of those postcards over a short period of time?

If I know of someone who might want to buy or sell, what's the best way for me to have them contact you?

It's always a good idea to have clear, concise responses prepared for your SOI. Practicing your scripts can make a big difference.

Summary

In closing, remember that your SOI is an excellent resource for leads to increase your real estate business. Remember, nearly half—49 percent!—of first-time home buyers said they found their agent through a recommendation or referral from a friend, family member, or neighbor (according to the 2006 National Association of REALTORS® Profile of Buyers and Sellers). Try implementing the 30/15 rule to contact your SOI throughout the year, and remember to concentrate more touches and communication efforts on the 20% group. For a real bang for your buck, you should contact your SOI in the early part of the year with a Power of 8 campaign, sending the same postcard to the same group of people over an 8 week period. Finally, keep a notebook handy or a running list in your smart phone or computer of your SOI for easy updating as you meet new friends and add business contacts throughout the year. By keeping your SOI prospecting activities going on a continuous basis, your business is sure to flourish and allow you a long and successful tenure as a real estate professional.

6 Working with Buyers

Many real estate professionals enjoy a more narrow focus with their real estate business in terms of what types of clients they work with. For example, some agents choose to work solely as buyer representatives or "buyer's agents." But many real estate professionals practice on both sides of the fence, working with buyers and sellers on a regular basis. Prospecting for buyers can be a challenging quest for many real estate agents. Generally, trying to find where the buyers are or how to get them is more difficult than finding potential sellers. To effectively find buyers, you may have to hold home-buyer seminars, send postcards to apartments or non-owner-occupied dwellings, and much more. Once you can zero in on where your buyers are coming from and how you can communicate with these buyers on a regular basis, your job as a real estate professional will be much easier. The following list contains some ways and ideas you might find helpful to reach potential buyers. Postcards, letters, flyers, etc., reflect these possible avenues for finding buyers.

- Apartments/renters
- Classified ads in the for-rent section
- Working open houses
- Working for-sale-by-owners (FSBOs) (they may need to buy after they sell)
- Working your sphere of influence (SOI)
- Home-buyer seminars
- Mailing lists geared to non-home-owners
- Lead generation programs through the Multiple Listing Service (MLS)
- Printed listings in flyer boxes (prospects picked up from other listings)
- *Free* report offers
- Relationships with mortgage loan officers
- Contacts with human resource directors at local firms and organizations
- Contacts with local chamber of commerce
- Name rides on top of for-sale signs

As you can see there is a wide variety of ways and places to find and work with buyers. This chapter will help you develop ideas and gives suggestions to locate these buyers, along with ways to follow-up and communicate with potential buyers on a regular basis. The final part of this chapter will help you build a buyer's presentation in either PowerPoint or on paper to help solidify your work as a real estate professional and to help encourage the buyer to maintain a commitment to you as the real estate professional in the home-buying process.

Staying in Touch

Staying in touch with buyers who inquire about listings is important. Normally you can send a thank you card or letter to the buyer you come into contact with, but the author believes that, with today's technology, speed is critical. If the buyer has an e-mail address, you might consider dropping him or her a short note electronically. The following is an e-mail example from my book *5 Minutes to a Great Real Estate Letter*, published by Thomson Learning; this e-mail example is also found on the CD-ROM included with this book.

509 East Main St.
Park Hills, MO 63601
Office: 573-756-0077
Cell: 573-760-4220 Fax: 573-756-1336
Email: John@RealEstateTechGuy.com
Website: www.RealEstateTechGuy.com

We're Not #1, You Are!

[Date]

«Address Block»

«Greeting Line»

Thank you for stopping by my real estate office this past week. I was curious as to how things went with the property you looked at for which I provided information. I will continue to search for properties that I feel might meet your needs. Please let me know if there is more information I can provide on any additional listings you have an interest in.

As always, thank you for allowing me the opportunity to be of service to you with your real estate needs, and I hope to hear from you soon.

Sincerely,

[Agent's Name]
[Agency Name]
[Web Address]
Mail to: [E-Mail Address]
[Phone] [Fax]
Licensed to practice real estate in [State]
[Quote or Slogan]

Saying thank you to your new customers is important, but communicating to them on a consistent basis is essential if you want to be remembered and set apart from other real estate agents. Enacting a drip marketing campaign can help serve the purpose of staying in touch with your new buyer. Remind yourself that most real estate agents fail to stay in touch with customers and clients on a regular basis.

The previous example shows how you could communicate with potential buyers through a drip marketing campaign using the "free" report at the end of this chapter entitled "Avoiding the Ten Biggest Pitfalls When Buying a Home." By incorporating a different tip each week through a postcard design, you would be able to contact the buyers over a 10 to 14 week period. The following table illustrates how you might consider implementing a drip marketing campaign to prospective buyers over a 12 week span.

Week	Type of Communication	Details
1	E-mail or direct mail	Send a thank you note for your initial meeting and/or showing of property
1	Phone Call	Follow-up with buyers on progress or desire to purchase home
2	Postcard	Tip #1—Pitfalls to avoid
3	Phone Call	Follow-up with buyers on progress or desire to purchase home
4	Postcard	Tip #2—Pitfalls to avoid
5	Postcard	Tip #3—Pitfalls to avoid
6	Phone Call	Follow-up with buyers on progress or desire to purchase home
6	Postcard	Tip #4—Pitfalls to avoid
7	Postcard	Tip #5—Pitfalls to avoid
8	Phone Call	Follow-up with buyers on progress or desire to purchase home
8	Postcard	Tip #6—Pitfalls to avoid
9	Postcard	Tip #7—Pitfalls to avoid
10	Postcard	Tip #8—Pitfalls to avoid
11	Postcard	Tip #9—Pitfalls to avoid
12	Phone Call	Follow-up with buyers on progress or desire to purchase home
12	Postcard	Tip #10—Pitfalls to avoid

Along with sending the ten-tips postcards and following up by phone, you should also be submitting information on new listings to the buyers by direct mail or by e-mail. Most MLSs have the capability for the agent to set up a saved search that will forward new listings to buyers the moment they become available in the MLS. Here's a good example of how you might advertise for new buyers by promoting this service from your MLS:

Don't Roll The Dice!

Let me set-up a customized search in our Multiple Listing Database to notify you of new listings when they become available.

Call me, John Mayfield at 573-760-XXXX to learn how you can be the "first" to know of new homes offered for-sale in our local Multiple Listing Service.

www.TheRealEstateTechGuy.com

Be The First to Know!

Let me set-up a customized search in our Multiple Listing Database to notify you of new listings when they become available.

Call me, John Mayfield at 573-760-XXXX to learn how you can be the "first" to know of new homes offered for-sale in our local Multiple Listing Service.

www.TheRealEstateTechGuy.com

The previous two postcard examples would work well for sending to apartment complexes in your local marketplace. The following letters could also be used to help with your marketing campaign to stay in touch and communicate with buyers. For more letters to use with buyer prospects, don't forget to check out *5 Minutes to a Great Real Estate Letter,* and for ad ideas refer to *5 Minutes to a Great Real Estate Ad.* You can purchase both books from www.5-Minutes.com.

509 East Main St.
Park Hills, MO 63601
Office: 573-756-0077
Cell: 573-760-4220 Fax: 573-756-1336
Email: John@RealEstateTechGuy.com
Website: www.RealEstateTechGuy.com

We're Not #1, You Are!

[Date]

«*Address Block*»

«*Greeting Line*»

Thank you for stopping by our office today regarding your interest in purchasing a new home. I hope that you found the information I provided you with helpful. Don't forget my Web site, *[agent or company Web site]*, where you can view additional properties for sale and download many helpful and *free* reports to guide you through the home-buying process.

Again, it was a pleasure meeting you, and I hope that I can be of service to you with your real estate needs. Feel *free* to call me if you have any questions.

Sincerely,

[Agent's Name]
[Agent's Title]

Letter for Phone Inquiry

509 East Main St.
Park Hills, MO 63601
Office: 573-756-0077
Cell: 573-760-4220 Fax: 573-756-1336
Email: John@RealEstateTechGuy.com
Website: www.RealEstateTechGuy.com

We're Not #1, You Are!

[Date]

«*Address Block*»

«*Greeting Line*»

Thank you for your phone call today regarding your interest in purchasing a new home. I hope that you found the information I provided you with helpful. Don't forget my Web site, *[agent or company Web site]*, where you can view additional properties for sale and download many helpful and "FREE" reports to guide you through the home-buying process.

Again, it was a pleasure speaking with you today by phone, and I hope that I can be of service to you with your real estate needs. Feel *free* to call me if you have any questions.

Sincerely,

[Agent's Name]
[Agent's Title]

E-Mail Inquiry about Property for Sale

509 East Main St.
Park Hills, MO 63601
Office: 573-756-0077
Cell: 573-760-4220 Fax: 573-756-1336
Email: John@RealEstateTechGuy.com
Website: www.RealEstateTechGuy.com

We're Not #1, You Are!

«*Greeting Line*»

Thank you for your e-mail today regarding your interest in purchasing a new home. I have provided a Web link for you to view more information about this property and to preview additional digital photos. If you need anything else about this listing, please do not hesitate to e-mail or call me. I can be reached at *[agent's phone number]*.

Again, thank you for the e-mail, and I hope that I can be of service to you with your real estate needs.

Sincerely,

[Agent's Name]
[Agency Name]
[Web Address]
Mail to: [E-Mail Address]
[Phone] [Fax]
Licensed to practice real estate in [State]
[Quote or Slogan]

E-Mail Follow-Up Inquiry with Buyer

509 East Main St.
Park Hills, MO 63601
Office: 573-756-0077
Cell: 573-760-4220 Fax: 573-756-1336
Email: John@RealEstateTechGuy.com
Website: www.RealEstateTechGuy.com

We're Not #1, You Are!

«*Greeting Line*»

Just a short note to follow up with you regarding your possible real estate needs. I would be happy to show you this home or any others you might be interested in. I know that purchasing a home can be a big decision and there are many areas buyers should be aware of. That's why I'm making this special report available at no charge entitled, *"Avoid the 10 Biggest Pit Falls When Buying a Home."* You can download this "FREE" report by visiting the following link: *[Web Address Link for Report]*.

Again, thank you for your recent e-mail, and please let me know if I can be of service to you with your real estate needs. I hope you'll download my "FREE" report today!

Sincerely,

[Agent's Name]
[Agency Name]
[Web Address]
Mail to: [E-Mail Address]
[Phone] [Fax]
Licensed to practice real estate in [State]
[Quote or Slogan]

Working with Buyers   79

The Buyer's Presentation

Today many real estate agents understand the importance of working with buyers and the value and contribution they can add to their business. Buyers are also more savvy consumers today and realize that many real estate professionals will and can represent them as a "buyer's agent." Because of representation and the need to work with a sole real estate agent, having a good presentation to share with your customer is important. Just like trying to get a new listing with a seller, representing a buyer through a buyer's agency is no different. You could, in essence, call this a "buyer's listing." Done correctly, and fully explained to the consumer, a buyer's agency agreement serves as a contract between you, the agent, and the consumer/client. Having a presentation in paper form or electronically through the use of Microsoft PowerPoint, the real estate agent can deliver a compelling and meaningful message about buyers' representation and the need for the consumer to work with one real estate agent—hopefully you!

The following points cover some of the facts and details you should consider including with your buyer's presentation:

1. The home-buying process.
2. Explain the current condition of the housing market.
3. Market specifics— average sales price, days on market, and list to sales price ratio.
4. The inventory of homes within your given area.
5. Explain how the MLS works.
6. Explain about FSBOs.
7. Informing your buyers about new construction.
8. What the buyers should do when looking at open houses, new homes for-sale, and other similar situations.
9. The sales contract and disclosures.
10. How much earnest money is appropriate and what the earnest money represents.
11. Getting preapproved for a loan.
12. What takes place between contract and closing?
13. What does the closing entail?
14. Information about yourself and your company.
15. Explain your goals for the transaction:
    a. Good price
    b. No hassle
    c. Close within the buyer's timeframe
16. Why it's important for the consumer to enter into a buyer's agency.

By creating a sample presentation in a program such as Microsoft PowerPoint, you will be ready to deliver your buyer's presentation electronically to consumers via the Web, e-mail, a laptop, or Table PC. You can also print your PowerPoint slides and bind them in a notebook or file binder to deliver a hard copy to your prospective clients. It's important to keep your slides short and to the point, allowing yourself the ability to use the pages as talking points to discuss with your customer. The following example shows a PowerPoint slide created for earnest money.

This PowerPoint slide covers the three necessary questions you will need to address with any potential buyer regarding earnest money: What is it? Why? How Much? As a real estate professional, you need to have answers to these questions and others when addressing the buying and selling public. Knowing how to respond and what to say when giving presentations or when faced with questions will help build confidence in your real estate career.

Summary

Working with buyers can be a rewarding and satisfying part of the real estate professional's career. Today many real estate agents specialize in working exclusively with buyers. There are many ways and creative ideas to locate buyer prospects, and having a predefined buyer's presentation to offer to consumers is beneficial in encouraging and explaining why a potential buyer should work with one real estate agent. Remember to communicate and stay in touch with buyer prospects quickly and on a regular basis. Like other prospects, those with whom you can build rapport and trust will likely work with you in the future to find their new home.

Avoiding the Ten Biggest Pitfalls when Buying a Home

1. Failing to have your real estate agent provide detailed market analysis on your home's, value
2. Failing to get a building inspection on the residence you are purchasing
3. Neglecting to have a full staked survey on the property you are purchasing
4. Making a low-ball offer and discouraging the seller from negotiating with you
5. Failing to get prequalified for a loan prior to making the offer to purchase
6. Not allowing enough time to complete all of the necessary building and title examinations and inspections
7. Neglecting to work with buyer's agent
8. Purchasing a FSBO or other real estate without the use of a real estate professional or attorney
9. Purchasing a parcel of real estate without obtaining title insurance
10. Obtaining a city inspection!

Although the items listed here are not a full and comprehensive list of pitfalls or mistakes buyers can make when purchasing a home, they are issues that come up from time to time and tend to be problem areas for many buyers. You can avoid having such situations by using the right real estate agent. That's why [agent's name] is available and ready to serve you. For a more comprehensive explanation about some of the issues listed in this report, call [agent's name] at [phone number] so that I can be more thorough in explaining how these areas can be a possible determent to your next home purchase. I would also love to visit with you and put you on my computerized real estate listing search through our Multiple Listing Service so that you can be the first to find out about new listings that become available. For more information visit my Web site at [Web address] or e-mail me at [e-mail address].

How to Save Thousands on Your Next Home Purchase

Although this is not a comprehensive list of everything that needs to be followed when deciding to purchase real estate, it is a list of important items that we have noticed at *[agency name]*, which can play a big role for most buyers.

- Use a REALTOR®! As members of the National Association of REALTORS®, each member adheres to a strict code of ethics that provides a wide variety of benefits for buyers and sellers. Not all real estate agents are members of the National Association of REALTORS®.

- Have your REALTOR® provide a detailed price evaluation of the property you are purchasing. In other words, make sure that your REALTOR® compares the property you are purchasing with other homes in the area that have been recently sold. Note: It is more important to examine recently sold properties than the current active listing inventory or the expired listings. It is still important to see what other homes are listed for or have been listed which have not sold but you really want to put your infancies on what the other sold listings like the property you are purchasing have sold for.

- Get a home inspection. Many times buyers will choose to purchase a home without having the home inspected by a qualified professional. Many times, if an inspection is performed in a timely manner, you can generally ask the seller to repair or fix the items in question or get an allowance deducted from the price of the home. If it is an issue that cannot be resolved, you may even be able to be relieved from your contractual obligations.

- Depending on state laws and statutes, you should enter into a suitable buyer's agency relationship with your REALTOR®. It is important to understand that agency issues can play a big role in the purchase or sale of a home. By having real estate agent work with you as a buyer's agent the agent is providing duties of obligations for you the buyer and not the seller or the seller's agent. Make certain that the real estate professional you have hired has a good, clear understanding of buyer's agency and how it operates before entering into any buyer's agency contract.

- Put down a good earnest money deposit. Often, buyers put very little earnest money down when negotiating the purchase of a home; unfortunately, to the seller it shows little commitment on your part as a buyer to purchase the home. A larger earnest money deposit shows your sincerity and your intent to complete the purchase and can be a big factor in the negotiating of the purchase price.

- Watch important time lines. With most real estate contracts to purchase real estate documents, there are important dates and time lines that must be followed— how quickly the home inspection must be completed, when to review the title work, how quickly your loan approval must be met, and more. A good buyer's agent acting on your behalf will follow these guidelines and make sure that you meet each and every time requirement. However, it is also good practice on your part as the buyer to make note of these dates, and times so that nothing is overlooked or missed. A good example of this might be the date on which you should complete your home inspection and the date on which you should complete all of your mechanical and structural inspections. The contract may provide for you to terminate the transaction if there is a major defect that cannot be corrected or fixed. If this inspection is not performed in a timely manner under the dates and times of the sales contract and no notice is provided to the seller or seller's, agent, there may be no remedy in the state law to terminate the transaction .

- Shop around for your home mortgage. Often buyers will go to only one lender to apply for a home loan before beginning any initial credit reporting or verification of other signed documents; with a lender, find out the interest rate, closing cost, and other fees associated with your home mortgage. You can also request that the lender reduce part of the closing cost or ask if any fees are negotiable. Generally lenders' fees are not set in stone and can be negotiated or removed from the cost of the loan. For example, some lenders will waiver the cost of a credit report or appraisal fee to encourage you to do business with their company, or, if your credit is good enough, and depending on your down payment, some lenders may even waiver all or part of their origination fees. The important point is for you as a purchaser to ask if any of the costs for the loan can be eliminated or discounted.

- Get a survey. Most title insurance policies in many states do not cover encroachment or survey boundary problems when they arise. After the closing it is generally too late to get help from the previous owner you purchased the home from unless they knew about it or had reason to believe there was an encroachment. Still, it could cost you thousands of dollars in legal fees to correct the problem or seek a realty in the right amount of time.

- Examine your title policy in a timely manner. Make sure that your buyer's agent and you review the title policy in a timely manner. As noted in previous bullet points above, there are certain dates and time lines that need to be followed to report any objections you might have with something attached to the real estate. You would not be happy about such as a restriction.

- Make sure the seller provides a detailed disclosure about the property. Most states now require the sellers to provide comprehensive seller disclosure statements about the real estate they are selling. This can help you as a buyer to determine what, if any, problems or issues the sellers have had with the real estate they are conveying.

- Ask the seller for copies of warranties on any appliances or work they have had performed. It is generally easier for the seller to find this information prior to closing than after the transaction has been completed. So any type of warranty question prior to the seller receiving his or her funds for their house is a good idea.

- Take your time before you purchase. It is always a good idea to look at some homes before making a purchase decision. Don't feel as though you have to buy the first home you look at. Comparing the one you are interested in with several others can help you determine if the value is where it should be for the home you would like to purchase.

Why Every Buyer Should Get a Home Inspection

This is not a comprehensive list of the needs for a home inspection, nor should this report be relied on solely for the purchase of your next home. It is just a guide that can help you understand the benefits for having a home inspection prior to your next real estate purchase.

- Most sales contracts provide for the buyer to perform various inspections on the property within so many days after signing the sales contract. By having a qualified and recommended home inspector look at the property under consideration, you have the opportunity to find any major or structural defects in advance of the home purchase. This inspection and notification of the issues at hand can allow you, the borrower, to either cancel or void the contract or request the seller to make the necessary repairs prior to signing any closing documents. Of course, state laws and the contract verbiage will dictate the final outcome, but it is important to make sure the party representing you in the transaction includes the opportunity to have a building inspection of the property you plan to purchase.

- The inspector will look for things you never dreamed of! Most building inspectors will look for a wide variety of items both structurally, mechanically, and visible to you and I, and items that are not visible during the normal inspection.

- The building inspector will provide you with a detailed report outlining the issues and problems that need to be corrected. It is important to use this detailed report when requesting corrections to the contract or in the case of major structural defects as it allows you the opportunity to terminate the contract. Of course, you will need to seek legal council on the verbiage in the contract before you can move forward on your decision. But a detailed report will normally be necessary to provide to the seller or seller's agent should this situation arise.

- Don't panic about everything. Remember, the building inspector's job is to find problems and issues with the sales contract. It is not critical that every detail pointed out in the contract be correct or repaired. Some minor issues listed in the inspection report may only take a half a day's work and a couple hundred dollars to correct. Although you should consult with your agent regarding the legalities of your detailed inspection report, don't feel that every listed item in the inspection is a cause for panic.

- Ask for recommendations. Prior to hiring a building inspector it is always a good idea to ask for recommendations and find out what the satisfaction level has been with the inspector's past clients. You can not only request recommendations from building inspectors themselves, but you can also ask the real estate agent you are working with to provide a list of buyers who may have used one particular inspector or another. By doing this, you're sure to find out the positive or negative reactions of those who have worked with a given building inspector.

- Ask to see if the inspector is a member of any national organization. Some groups such as the American Society of Home Inspectors (ASHI) require the inspector to meet certain criteria and to have a certain educational background to be certified as one of their inspectors. This rigorous requirement assures you that the inspector you are hiring meets all of the qualification criteria and the code for performing a home inspection for you; it also assures you that inspectors are recertifying themselves on a continuous and regular basis so that they are constantly updated and familiar with the current building codes and construction requirements.

- A home inspection is not all that you will need. Although most home inspectors do a good job finding areas in need of repair and problem issues with the home you are planning to purchase, some cities and government municipalities require a separate occupancy inspection and permit prior to your moving into your future residence. Just because the building inspector investigates your home and finds little or no problem areas occasionally the city inspector may have a newly updated list and will require certain changes to be made to the home. Although most building inspectors will try to stay on top of these local city changes, occasionally one issue or area may fall through the cracks. It is not only a good idea to hire a building inspector but also to sign the necessary forms and documents and pay any local municipality fees so that the occupancy inspector can preview the home too.

- Don't forget local utility inspections. As noted in the previous bullet point for obtaining any local municipality occupancy inspections, it is also a good idea to have the local utility companies inspect the home for their standards required in turning on the utilities. Again, most inspectors do a good job looking at the utility requirements necessary during their home inspection. But occasionally the local gas company or electric company could have a requirement the building inspector is not aware of. It is always a good idea to cover all of your bases prior to closing so that an issue or problem does not arise after the seller has received the money and the contract dates have elapsed.

- Ask building inspectors what areas they do not cover and what additional inspections you might need. For example, some building inspectors are qualified to inspect for termites while others may not be. It is a good idea to make sure you know in advance what areas the inspector will not guarantee under his or her inspection.

- Order your inspection in advance. Remember the sales contract will have important dates for you to follow to request changes to the home that are in the sales contract. Please seek advice from your legal council or qualified real estate professional regarding these dates. But understand that waiting until the last minute can be detrimental and possibly cost you thousands of dollars if an issue or problem needs to be corrected and your inspection period has expired.

All the above bullet points do not form a complete list of items that could arise regarding building inspections, but they are a good guide for you to use and remember prior to purchasing your next home. At *[agency name]* we would love to help you with your next home purchase. I have additional *free* reports listed on my Web site at *[web address]*, and you can also call me at *[agent's phone number]* for more information. I hope this report has been helpful for you, and I look forward to hearing from you soon. *[agent's name]*

7 Working with Sellers

Ideas and Thoughts on Communicating With Your Listing Clients

Early in my career I heard a retired real estate salesperson make the following statement: *"Listing is existing!"* During my 28+ years as a real estate professional, I too can attest to this statement and how true it is to have a good listing inventory (products) as a real estate agent. If you've never heard this before, believe me when I say that listing is the key to success and longevity as a real estate professional!

There are numerous ways to get more listings as a real estate agent as discussed throughout the text: for-sale-by-owners, expired listings, and many other areas. This chapter will specifically deal with communicating to the seller on an ongoing basis once the listing contract has been signed and secured and your marketing efforts are to begin. We'll also discuss ideas and alternative marketing pieces that could be included with a listing presentation; however, the main objective and goal of this chapter is to provide resources to use for staying in touch with your client.

Ready to Market

After your listing contract is signed, it's now time to begin the marketing efforts for your client. In Real Estate 101, or any basic real estate prelicense course, the real estate agent learns the fiduciary obligations owed to the client. A commonly referred to acronym used for these fiduciary duties is C.O.A.L.D.:

C—Care
O—Obedience
A—Accounting
L—Loyalty
D—Disclosure

Making sure that you have a good marketing plan for your client and a systematic action plan for staying in touch with your listing client during the listing period is a big part of your fiduciary obligation to your client. A good place to begin your new product and your job at hand is to familiarize yourself with a checklist of items you need to secure and follow-up on for your seller. The following illustration details a sample checklist (also included on the enclosed CD-ROM) to use for this process. Feel free to add or make changes to the checklist to use with your daily business.

Checklist for Agents after the Home is Listed

- Input data into Multiple Listing Service (MLS) or onto company forms
- Submit all forms and information to main office
- Upload all photos to MLS
- Input data and upload photos to company Web site
- Input data and upload photos to agent Web site
- Input data and upload photos to www.realtor.com
- Place for-sale sign on property
- Add flyer box in front of home
- Send sellers copies of documents
- Send sellers thank you cards or letters for listing (see attached thank you letter)
- If referral is from a friend, send a thank you card or letter (see attached thank you letter)
- Prepare advertising copy (see *5 Minutes to a Great Real Estate Ad* for more help with this)
- Update any MLS or Web site remarks
- Prepare flyers for flyer box
- Notify top 20 agents in your marketplace about new listing (see attached letter)
- Notify neighbors about new listing (see attached letter)
- Set open-house date (if applicable)
- Set agent tour dates with office or other offices (if applicable)
- Install lock box
- Add information to the monthly letter you send to clients on your sphere of influence (SOI) list
- Send checklist entitled "Now That Your Home is Listed" to sellers
- Set up a seller action plan for this listing

Checklist for Sellers

Now That Your Home is Listed

- Make sure the lawn is mowed and trimmed on a regular basis!
- Remove any outside debris or other items which may give a cluttered appearance
- Wash all windows inside and out
- Keep your home straightened and picked up regularly
- Clean hardwood floors with buffer or high-gloss polish. (Make sure the floors do not become too slick for visitors.)
- Keep carpets vacuumed on a regular basis
- Make sure all beds are made

- Remove and put away any laundry items that may be lying around
- Be sure to keep clutter to a minimum!
- Paint the front door if needed
- Spruce up the front entrance and walkway for good first impressions
- Reduce and or remove any extra furniture so all rooms have a spacious feel
- Make sure all rooms have light, neutrally painted walls
- Open all blinds and draperies when property is shown to prospects
- Turn on all lights for showings to potential prospects
- Turn off all radios, television sets, and music during showings
- Remove jewelry and other important items prior to showings
- Replace all light bulbs
- Grease any squeaky doors or doorknobs as needed

Of course, there are many other items you may incorporate for a new listing according to your location and custom, and the checklists in the CD-ROM are fully editable for removal, addition, or other changes. Please note that you will need Microsoft Word to open and edit the documents.

509 East Main St.
Park Hills, MO 63601
Office: 573-756-0077
Cell: 573-760-4220 Fax: 573-756-1336
Email: John@RealEstateTechGuy.com
Website: www.RealEstateTechGuy.com

We're Not #1, You Are!

[Date]

«Address Block»

«Greeting Line»

Thank you so much for allowing me the opportunity to market your real estate. I want you to know that I count it an honor and privilege to be your real estate agent in this transaction. Over the next several days you will receive several postcards from me detailing some of the things to expect during the initial days of the listing period.

Please feel free to call me at any time if you have questions during the listing period. You can reach me at *[agent's phone number]*.

Our main goal at *[company name]* is to help you get the most money for your property in the shortest time frame possible with the fewest, if any, problems. We will be working diligently to make these goals a reality for you and for us.

Again, thank you for the opportunity to be of service to you with your real estate needs.

Sincerely,

[Agent's Name]
[Agent's Title]

509 East Main St.
Park Hills, MO 63601
Office: 573-756-0077
Cell: 573-760-4220 Fax: 573-756-1336
Email: John@RealEstateTechGuy.com
Website: www.RealEstateTechGuy.com

We're Not #1, You Are!

[Date]

«Address Block»

«Greeting Line»

Enclosed you will find a sample marketing fact sheet about your property I am making available to potential buyers when they inquire about your home. Please look over the information and feel free to let me know if you have any corrections or additions to the brochure.

As always, thank you for allowing me the opportunity to be of service to you with your real estate needs.

Sincerely,

[Agent's Name]
[Agent's Title]

The following page shows a sample marketing flyer created with the HP Real Estate Marketing Assistant Software (REMA). As noted earlier, one idea may be to send a series of postcards to your new listing clients over a 1 or 2 week period, covering some of the basic tips to be prepared for while the property is listed. The next series of illustrations show a few examples of how this marketing idea might work.

What to Expect Now That Your Home is Listed...

As always, "thank you" for your business?

Now that your home is listed for-sale, here's what is taking place. Information about your home is being transferred to the following sites:

☐ Our Local Multiple Listing Service
☐ Company Web Site
  o www.MayfieldRE.com
☐ Agent Web site
  o www.RealEstateTechGuy.com
☐ Advertising copy prepard for the local newspaper

Please know that we are doing everything possilbe to help bring a "SOLD" sign soon for you.

Country Charm

With this Victorian 2-Story Home on 71 Acres...

Features

- 4 Bedrooms

- 3 ½ Baths

- Full Finished Basement

- Gourmet Kitchen with all appliances

- Wrap-around Porch

- Large patio area with Hot Tub

- Small pond

- White vinyl fencing

- Great views

- And much more…

- Priced at $950,000

You'll appreciate all of the charm and beauty this home has to offer. Located only minutes from town, you will enjoy the best of both worlds. Country living and fresh air with convenient access to city shopping.

For a private showing, contact John Mayfield today!

John Mayfield GRI, CRB, ABR
509 East Main St.
Park Hills, MO 63601

Office: 573-756-0077
Fax: 573-756-1336
Cell: 573-760-4220
Email:
John@RealEstateTechGuy.com
Website:
www.RealEstateTechGuy.com

The following descriptions detail a copy that could be used over a 7 day mailing period of "What to Expect" postcards. You can find this copy on the enclosed CD-ROM, and you can copy and paste it inside of your postcard mailings if you choose to do so.

Day One

Now that your home is listed for sale, here's what is taking place. Information about your home is being transferred to the following sites:

Our local Multiple Listing Service
Company Web site
www.MayfieldRE.com
Agent Web site
www.RealEstateTechGuy.com
Advertising copy prepared for the local newspaper
Please know that we are doing everything possilbe to help bring a "SOLD" sign soon for you.

Day Two

A for-sale sign and lock box along with property flyers will be installed at your property to aid in selling your real estate. Should the for-sale sign disappear or the marketing flyers run out at any time, let me know, and I will have them replaced immediately.

Please know that we are doing everything possible to bring a "SOLD" sign soon for you.

Day Three

A home-marketing book will be developed and delivered to your property with detailed information. This book should be kept on your kitchen counter and available when your home is shown to prospective buyers.

Please know that we are doing everything possible to bring a "SOLD" sign soon for you.

Day Four

Postcards to the top 20 agents in our board will be mailed, informing them of your property and the many benefits it offers to potential buyers.

Please know that we are doing everything possible to bring a "SOLD" sign soon for you.

Day Five

Postcards to the local neighborhood will be sent out, providing people with detailed information should they know of a friend or family member who may be interested moving to the area.

Please know that we are doing everything possible to bring a "SOLD" sign soon for you.

Day Six

Agent open-house for local offices will be set up for the upcoming week. I will work with you on a date and time that is convenient for you regarding the agent open-house.

Please know that we are doing everything possible to bring a "SOLD" sign soon for you.

Day Seven

General public open-house will be set up and scheduled to help get potential buyers into your home as soon as possible. I will work with you on a date and time that is convenient to you regarding the public open-house.

Please know that we are doing everything possible to bring a "SOLD" sign soon for you.

Remember that my book *5 Minutes to a Great Real Estate Letter*, published by Thomson Learning, offers a wide variety of letters and information you can use to communicate with your seller clients on a consistent basis. You will also find my book *5 Minutes to a Great Real Estate Ad*, also published by Thomson Learning, a valuable resource to save time and money in creating advertising copy for newspapers, Web sites, or your Multiple Listing copy. You can also purchase these books from www.5-Munites.com.

The following page shows a "Monthly Marketing" update available from my book *5 Minutes to a Great Real Estate Letter*.

Monthly Marketing Update Form

Date Completed	Description of Activity	Cost

For: Owner Name _____ Office/MLS # _____

Property Address _____

Once you have listings to sell, you'll need to write and prepare advertising copy for your new listings. With my book *5 Minutes to a Great Real Estate Ad*, you can prepare and write advertising, Multiple Listings, and Internet Web copy in a snap. Here are two examples from my book on how the advertising copy was implemented—one as normal classified ad copy and the other through the use of a postcard sent to a group of potential prospects.

> ***Enjoy the Good Life*** *with this «Bedrooms» bedroom «Baths» bath «Style_of_Home» home located minutes from town. Over «Acres» cleared acres makes this a place to make your dreams come true! Extra features included are «Feature_1», «Feature_2», and «Feature_3». For more information, call «Listing_Agent» at «Phone_Number». «Listing_Code_Number»*
> *(Ad #17)*

This Victorian farmhouse is situated on its own five-acre parcel of land. Gorgeous shade trees abound on the property with lots of flowers and several small water gardens. Spacious rooms and fully restored. You can't go wrong with this new listing! For a private tour, call «Listing_Agent» at «Phone_Number» or e-mail «Listing_Agent» at «Listing_Agent_Email». «Listing_Code_Number»

The advertising copy works with a Microsoft Excel Spreadsheet so that all of the information details about your listing are inserted into the proper merge fields.

Home-Marketing Book

Having a "home-marketing book" is a good idea to prepare for your listing clients. A home-marketing book helps consumers with questions they may have while looking at the property you have for sale. Some agents will have enough copies of the following information that a buyer or their agent could take copies with them if need be. If you desire to provide extra copies for potential buyers or agents, you might indicate so on the front cover of your book.

Using clear protective sheet covers is a good way to have your information included with the book along with extra copies.

The following pages show a sample cover letter to include with your home-marketing book and possible ideas of information that can be added to your book. Normally it's a good idea for your sellers to leave this book on the kitchen countertop and be made available whenever the property is being shown.

509 East Main St.
Park Hills, MO 63601
Office: 573-756-0077
Cell: 573-760-4220 Fax: 573-756-1336
Email: John@RealEstateTechGuy.com
Website: www.RealEstateTechGuy.com

We're Not #1, You Are!

[Date]

«Address Block»

Dear Real Estate Colleague and Potential Home Buyer,

Thank you for taking time out of your busy schedule for previewing my listing at *[property address]*. I've taken the time to prepare this "Home-Marketing Book" for your convenience and to help answer any questions you may have while looking at this property. In this home-marketing book you'll find information such as a fact sheet, disclosures, and information I have gathered from my own research and the seller's help. I believe you'll find this a warm and comfortable home, and you will be able to create and share many memories here over the years.

Feel free to have your agent contact me with any additional information or questions you may have.

Again, the owners of the property and I appreciate you taking time out to preview this listing, and I hope you find the information helpful.

Sincerely,

[Agent's Name]
[Agent's Title]

Some other information you might consider including with your home-marketing book are:

- Fact sheet about property
- Disclosures (seller's disclosure and lead-based paint, if applicable)
- Any other required state or local disclosure forms— city inspection, etc.
- Photos (seasonal views of homes if available from sellers)
- Survey or plat
- Copies of recent expenditures and or improvements
- Utility bills or summary or average of utility costs
- What we'll miss most! (have sellers give list of things they'll miss the most about their home)
- Copy of tax records
- Information about construction of home, insulation R-factor, wall thickness, etc.
- Date of major home improvements–roof, carpet, air-conditioning, etc.
- Any warranties or information regarding appliances, heating and cooling, water heater
- Copies of restrictions or subdivision regulations, zoning ordinances, or other information affecting title to the property
- Copy of building inspection if completed
- Copy of appraisal if completed
- Copy of other inspections such as city occupancy
- Copy of well and septic certifications
- Copy of previous title commitment

As you can see, we have a long and exhaustive list of items that could be included with your home-marketing book. Although not all of these items are a must to be included, many can help answer potential questions the buyer or agent may have, helping to eliminate concerns or issues in advance. Generally most buyers and agents find a nicely prepared home-marketing book an asset when they view a home. It's also a great way to demonstrate your professional marketing abilities as a real estate agent and how you conduct business when selling properties for your clients.

Just Listed

Sending out "Just Listed" postcards to your SOI and/or the neighbors is an excellent idea to generate leads and potential buyers. The following example shows a sample postcard (front and back) created with the HP Real Estate Marketing Assistant Software (REMA) and ad copy from my book *5 Minutes to a Great Real Ad*.

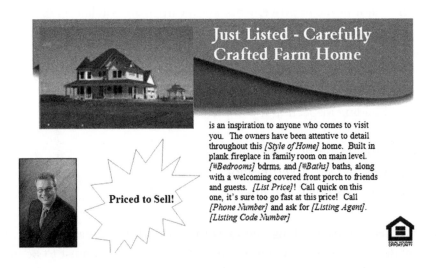

You might also consider creating a group of business cards for your client to hand out to potential buyers, other friends, and family members. After all, most sellers who want to sell their home quickly will be willing to pass out information and cards to others they know who might be considering a new home purchase. Here's a sample template of how you could take a photo of the client's home, add details about the property, and print out two or three sheets (20 to 30 business cards) for your clients to distribute to potential home buyers. You might also consider adding your photo, name, and contact information on the back. You can find this template on the enclosed CD-ROM.

Copy goes here!

Add more copy here

Copy goes here!

Add more copy here

Copy goes here!

Add more copy here

Copy goes here!

Add more copy here

Copy goes here!

Add more copy here

Copy goes here!

Add more copy here

Copy goes here!

Add more copy here

Copy goes here!

Add more copy here

Free Reports

11 Ways to Get Your House in Tip Top Shape Prior to Selling It!

And Maximize the Most Income!

Many people want to know what the secret is to getting the most out of their real estate in order to appeal to most consumers looking for real estate today. This report will guide you through many of the things that can help get the most dollars when selling your property.

1. Paint the interior. Most buyers appreciate a good fresh coat of paint, and this will help enhance your property's value. It will also help brighten your rooms, giving them a new, clean appearance. Stay away from bold and bright colors and focus more on lighter and softer earth-toned shades. This will also help make the rooms feel larger and appeal to a larger group of potential buyers.

2. Paint the outside. Curb appeal is important, and there is nothing worse for a real estate professional than to try and market a home that is in desperate need of painting. Of course, depending on the time of year and the weather conditions, if at all possible, paint the exterior. As noted with the suggestion for interiors of using soft, lighter, neutral colors, do the same for painting the outside of your home. Stay away from bright colors that others may not like.

3. Pick Up Any Outside Debris, Trash, or Clutter. First impressions make a huge impact on potential buyers. Should your property have unwanted clutter when shown initially to consumers, it will not help in the marketing and selling of your home. A few hours of hard raking, cleaning, and picking up odds and ends could add thousands to the sales price of your home.

4. Reduce Extras and Odds and Ends From Your Home. Rooms with too much furniture or too many decorations can often detract from the showing of your home. Usually too much décor can make the rooms look smaller and hurt your chances of selling your home. Put away unwanted furniture or items that you can do without during the marketing stage of your property listing. Your goal is to make your property look spacious and comfortable. Buyers also want to see rooms that appear spacious to them.

5. Be Sure to Open Blinds and Draperies. This is a great idea to aid the salesperson in selling your home. When your property is in tip top shape and ready to show, having as much light as possible helps brighten your home and give it a good feel.

6. Avoid Playing Music. Although you may like the music playing in the background, it can be a deterrent to the agent and buyers while looking at your home. Keep music off while your home is being shown.

7. Price Your Property Right From The Beginning. Many buyers take the approach and attitude that they can always come down on price. This can be a bad thing to do. Many buyers feel that if a home has been listed for a long time there is something wrong with it. Most agents will tell you that the best activity occurs during the first 2 to 3 weeks of the listing begin date. After a few weeks, the activity will begin to taper off and showings will cease. If your home is priced incorrectly from the beginning, it will not get a lot of showings, and the longer your home is on the market, the more buyers will feel that it's tainted or something's wrong. Price your home right from the beginning to help get the most activity and a quicker sale.

8. Have Your Carpets Cleaned. It's a good idea to have your carpets cleaned or your hardwood floors polished or waxed. This is normally not too expensive and can usually add a lot of appeal to potential buyers.

9. Hire a Staging Company. If possible, hire a staging company to help show you ways to maximize the room appeal and value of your residence. Many real estate firms have a staging company or staff who can aid in this service. Feel free to ask me about how I can help with staging, too.

10. Purchase New Linens and Towels for Bathrooms. This can help in giving a new appearance to your bathrooms.

11. Consider Wallpapering. Be careful here, and do not use bold or daring papers; use a basic, light, general theme when wallpapering. Dark colors make rooms look smaller, and you need to stay away from any colors that may make the room look small or busy.

How to Save Thousands on Your Next Home Sale

Are you thinking about selling your house or another parcel of real estate that you own? If so, it is important to follow some of these guidelines to help you get the most out of your real estate and possibly save you thousands of dollars in the future. Although this is not a comprehensive list of everything that needs to be followed when deciding to sell your real estate, it is a list of important items that we have noticed at *[agency name]* which can play a big role for most sellers.

- Make sure you list your property with a REALTOR®. As members of the National Association of REALTORS®, each member adheres to a strict code of ethics that provide a wide variety of benefits for buyers and sellers. Not all real estate agents are members of the National Association of REALTORS®.

- Have your real estate agent perform a competitive market analysis. Often, real estate agents will not have the information or expertise and know-how to learn what other properties have sold for or what your current competition is. A real estate agent working for you will prepare a competitive Comparable Market Analysis so that you can look at what other properties have sold for and what other properties similar to yours are listed for.

- Price your property competitively and correctly from the beginning! Many sellers want to try and get the most out of their property and adopt the philosophy that they can always adjust the price at a later date. In reality, the best and most qualified prospects will come early in the game, when the for-sale sign first goes up, and your property first hits the local Multiple Listing Service hot sheet. Often, sellers who price their property higher in the beginning and then begin to lower their price over time get less for their property than they would have if it had been priced correctly from the beginning.

- Get a home inspection in advance. Normally a home inspection will not cost you a lot of money and can be a good marketing tool for your agent when selling your property. Inspections are also good because any major issues or problems that might arise can be fixed in advance. Smaller items that can sometimes give the buyer bargaining room to reduce cost can also be prepared or fixed in advance of your marketing efforts and can generally save you hundreds if not thousands of dollars.

- Reduce clutter. It is important to remember that reducing clutter and as much furniture and other items in advance can help in the sale of your property. If you need to store things in boxes or pack things up and move them to another location or to another family member or friend's property, the extra room can normally be a benefit.

- Give your home a fresh coat of paint. Generally a fresh coat of paint and cleaning of the carpets are all very important in helping you sell your property. Normally, painting your home will not cost much money and can add a good, fresh appeal to prospective residents.

- Open the drapes and turn on lights. It is always a good idea to allow as much light to infiltrate your property as possible. Turning on lights, adding new, stronger light bulbs, and opening blinds and drapes is a big plus for marketing your property.

- Avoid music, and avoid being home when your property is shown. Although many sellers like to be present during the showing of their property, for a real estate agent your absence can help immensely in the marketing of your property. Buyers normally feel more free to open closets and look at the property without sellers following them around or talking too much about the property. You might also give the wrong information or come off as desperate to sell by being present during the showing.

- Provide copies of receipts on items you have purchased for your agent or repairs you have made over the last couple of years. If you have installed a new roof and you have a copy of how much you spent for the roof, that information can be helpful to put in a folder or book along with any other major expenses or expenditures you have had. It is also a good idea to have copies of your taxes, insurance premiums, utility costs per month, and any other important information, such as surveys or plats, that may be available to help your real estate agent during the marketing process.

- Clean the front porch and front lawn of any debris or items that might be a turn off when people are driving by to look at your property. Making sure your lawn is mowed and well-manicured, along with a cleanly swept front porch without a lot of debris, is very important in the marketing efforts of your property.

- Make your home look like one in a magazine. Having your beds made, clothes picked up off the floor, tables straightened, and rooms fit for a picture in a magazine is important and can be a big hit when buyers tour your property for a possible home purchase.

- Be open to suggestions from your agent. It is always important to remember that your real estate agent is the professional and has the expertise or know-how to sell your property. Many agents will report back to your listing agent as to what buyers or other agents think about your property or what needs to be fixed or changed. If this is the case, be sure to have an open mind and listen to any suggestions that your agent may have to improve the market ability of your property.

Again, this is not a comprehensive list of what you need to do to sell your property, but incorporating these few suggestions will help immensely in the marketing of your property and get you the most out of your real estate for a happy and successful real estate closing. For more information about any *[agency name]* listings visit our website at *[agency Web site]*. You can also e-mail us if you have other questions at *[agent's e-mail]*.

Ten Things that will Aid in the Marketing of Your Home

1. Make a "I'll Miss List!" There are several items you'll probably miss when you leave your house. These items are normally excellent marketing features to promote to potential buyers. Take time to make note of the things you enjoy and will miss when the sale is completed and you've moved from your house. Items you appreciate are items someone else will enjoy too!

2. Know the Facts! Most buyers will have questions about taxes, lot size, utility costs, and other pertinent information about your property. It's always a good idea to know the facts and to have this information available for potential consumers looking at your real estate. Take time to research this information and have it readily available for buyers and or real estate agents.

3. Recent Repairs. Most borrowers need to know about any recent updates, repairs, or additions you've made to your home. For example, a new roof, furnace or central air, and water heater are all important to note. If so, what was the cost, when was it installed, and who did the work are all noteworthy features to have for buyers and agents when selling your property. Any items of repair or newly added during your tenure should be listed on a separate sheet if at all possible. It's also a good idea to furnish copies of paid receipts if you choose on the items repaired or installed to validate these costs. Sometimes placing this information in a binder is a good marketing feature to show buyers and agents.

4. Replace Light Bulbs. Changing light bulbs to a higher wattage can be an aid in brightening rooms and giving a more spacious feel to your rooms. Always check the light fixture and the maximum wattage and do not add bulbs above the recommended usage. You can also add a drop of vanilla extract to bulbs on lamps to aid in providing a fresh smell to rooms if needed.

5. Remove Any Heirlooms or Keepsakes. Many times sellers will want to keep certain items that have sentimental value to them such as a light fixture or wall mirror that has been affixed to the real property. If you have an item that you plan to replace, then you should do so prior to any showing. Once buyers visit your property and begin making offers to purchase your property, it's generally hard to negotiate these items off of the offer to purchase.

6. Clean the Gutters and Add Extensions Where Needed. You never know when your property may be shown, and if it's raining that day, the last thing you want to portray is a house in which the water is gushing over the gutters and downspouts. Making sure the gutters are cleaned and extensions move the water away from your foundation is always a good idea for continued maintenance of your home and shows buyers your commitment to caring for your home and keeping it in tip top shape.

7. Hire a Building Inspector. Let's face it—you want to sell your home. If so, it's probably not a bad idea to have a building inspector look at your home and make a list of repairs or items that need to be fixed prior to marketing your property. After all, many homebuyers will have a home inspection too; so this type of preinspection will help fix in advance any potential problems a future inspector might have to correct. Many buyers will also get "cold" feet if the inspector shows too many needed repairs on their report. By fixing these issues in advance you can ward off these potential future problems.

8. Be Patient. Don't panic if your home is not shown during the first week or two. Sometimes it may take a while for your home to get lookers and/or offers. The market can be up or down at any given time, and so when your home is not shown, do not think there is something wrong.

9. Communication. Good communication between you and me is important. Advise me of any changes, additions, or problems that should be noted or update on the seller's disclosure. I, in turn, will promise to keep you abreast of the conditions and market changes to the local real estate economy.

10. Stay out of the way. Although many sellers have good intentions when there home is shown to aid in the presentation of the property, it can often be a distraction and makes it harder for the real estate agent to do their job. If at all possible, try to stay out of the way when your property is being shown.

Summary

Remember that staying in touch with your clients is an integral part of your job as a real estate agent. You have a fiduciary obligation to your clients, and making sure you implement C.O.A.L.D. is important if you expect to win repeat business and referrals from your clients.

Learn how to create home-marketing books, postcards, flyers, and business cards for your clients to promote their property for sale. And finally, educate your clients on what to expect when selling their home. There are several reports included with this book to help you explain the home-selling process to your clients that should help make your job a little easier.

8 Agent Promotion

Introduction

Prior to the mid-1980s and 1990s, real estate agents dealt primarily with the marketing of properties or homes for sale. At the ripe old age of 47 (smiling) I love to refer to the old days of selling real estate. As my biography in this book indicates, I received my real estate license at the age of 18. In those days real estate agents' primary concern was in marketing and selling houses. Although many real estate professionals were developing a name for themselves in their marketplace, few if any were concentrating on creating a brand around themselves. Now, that philosophy has changed. Today, real estate professionals must not only market houses but must also learn to market and promote themselves. Trying to stand out among the crowd and being remembered in your marketplace as the real estate guru is essential if you want to achieve success. With companies such

as Hobbs Herder, who deal primarily with the promotion and marketing of agents and offices, today's marketing goes much deeper and wider than just including the marketing of homes for sale. Being effective and successful at marketing yourself as a real estate agent (agent promotion) is as much a part of marketing as the promotion of homes for sale. It's almost as though you have a double-edged sword as a real estate agent trying to attend to both the marketing of yourself and your client's properties. Creating a brand or logo for yourself is generally a good way to differentiate yourself from the competition. Why is it so important to market yourself as a real estate agent in today's competitive business environment? Because, if you choose to remain neutral or similar to all of the other real estate agents in your marketplace, it will be difficult for consumers to remember you as a real estate professional when they have real estate needs.

Chances are you'll blend in with all the other real estate agents in your marketplace and miss out on the extra business. Think for a minute about various real estate agents in your marketplace who are successful and/or who are using creative marketing gimmicks to help draw attention to their real estate business. Are you able to think of someone? If so, what are they doing that has caused you to remember them? Probably the reason you could think of them so quickly is because they're doing something different that is out of the norm. Promoting yourself as an agent is an important part of the marketing process if you want to move your career to a new and higher level. However, coming up with a gimmick or new idea is never a good thing if it's promoting a brand or an image that isn't you. For example, my logo and branding as a real estate speaker is tailored around the "real estate tech guy." I chose this image and brand because I love technology! My colleagues enjoy hearing me speak about technology and how it's implemented in the real estate business.

For me, the real estate tech guy is a win–win situation. I'm using and promoting a theme that I love and have a passion for, and my audience reacts positively to my training seminars. For someone else who is not as excited about technology as I am, using this theme would not be a good idea. Therefore, remember point number one, when building an image or logo/theme about your career—choose something you're passionate about! Trains, cooking, golf, or hiking. Make sure your logo and image is built around your passion!

Next, evaluate the need for your brand and/or marketing niche you plan to use in your promotion. For example, you wouldn't want to be a luxury home specialist if there were very few luxury homes for sale in your marketplace.

Finally, don't be afraid to draw on your experiences from previous employment or any other experience you have had. This is a good way to jump-start your proposed marketing plan as a real estate professional. In working with other people who are going through a transition such as a divorce or the loss of a loved one, you can use your experience if you have had a similar one.

It's not a requirement to have a specialized niche, logo, or theme to be a success in the real estate business, but it does help in setting you apart from the average real estate professionals in your marketplace. If you're not able to develop a logo or theme at an affordable cost, then you might consider agent promotion without a logo or theme. However, always include a photo, slogan, or mission statement and other pertinent information in all of your ads and marketing efforts.

Your Target Market

Imagine for a moment that you're walking down your favorite grocery store isle. There's a product you need to purchase that is normally not on your regular grocery item list. As your eyes move across the shelves to the various brands of the product—which item do you choose? For some people, price is the important factor. Others may rely heavily on packaging or the looks and style of the container the product is in. Others are searching for the product they've heard about through advertising or word of mouth. Finally, some of the shoppers looking for this grocery item are looking for the name of the product as referred by a friend. A small percentage will pick up the product on impulse, but most people are driven by the product packaging, style, price, or word of mouth from someone else. In his book *The Tipping Point,* Malcomb Gladwell discusses the Law of Fundamental Attribution Error

(FAE). What Gladwell points out about the Law of FAE is that consumers tend to make decisions on general observations rather than facts. The following information is from an article titled "Why law and economics' perfect rationality should not be traded for behavioral law and economics' equal incompetence" by Gregory Mitchell in the *Georgetown Law Journal* of November 2002:

> *Richard Nisbett & Lee Ross, Human Inference: Strategies and Shortcomings of Social Judgment 31 (1980); see also Daniel T. Gilbert & Patrick S. Malone, The Correspondence Bias, 117 Psychol. Bull. 21, 21 (1995)*
>
> *("Three decades of research in social psychology have shown that many of the mistakes people make are of a kind: When people observe behavior, they often conclude that the person who performed the behavior was predisposed to do so-that the person's behavior corresponds to the person's unique dispositions-and they draw such conclusions even when a logical analysis suggests they should not."); Douglas S. Krull et al.,*

In other words, for most consumers, perception is reality! If you're doing a good job marketing yourself and standing out among the crowd, then you will probably get noticed and people will remember you as the person to do real estate with in your community, even if you're not selling a lot during the early days of your major promotions. The Law of FAE works for the real estate agent who has more signs up around town, advertises more, and is a bit more clever, or is noticed throughout the real estate marketplace by means of advertising, promotion, and other resources. People will draw a positive conclusion about you and your real estate career even if a logical analysis of the situation would tell them something different.

The following photos show a real estate agent from [area], MO, who worked for me, Paul Pinkston. Paul developed a theme around the slogan "Paul works hard." Paul registered the URL www.PaulWorksHard.com and stenciled it onto a Volkswagen automobile he used with his real estate business. This was a huge success for Paul and helped him increase market share and put his real estate career at a new level. Paul used the Law of FAE to its fullest, making consumers believe he was a big player in the real estate industry early on even when he was not. The neat thing is that it only took Paul a short time until he indeed was one of the major real estate players in our community.

Paul used many clever and unique ideas to help build his business and get noticed by consumers in his local marketplace.

New-Agent Marketing Ideas

Although implementing any idea found throughout the chapters of this book would be beneficial and a good way for you to build your business, the following pages provide ideas for a new or existing agent to build their business through agent promotion.

New-Agent Action Plan

- Develop your sphere of influence (SOI) list (minimum of 100 people).
- Get a good photo taken.
- Order business cards and other supplies needed.
- Put your SOI into computer software database.
- Develop a brand image or logo.
- Create personalized stationery.
- Register a URL such as www.JohnDMayfield.com.
- Set up an e-mail address for the registered URL.
- Prepare an introductory letter to send to your SOI (see letter in this chapter).
- Develop a tri-fold brochure about yourself.
- Create a business plan.
- Create a marketing plan.
- Develop a listing presentation.
- Develop a buyer's presentation.
- Create an agent resume.
- Create a company resume.
- Prepare a sample "home-marketing" sellers' book.
- Personalize "*free*" reports with all relevant information.
- Prepare a for-sale-by-owner (FSBO) presentation kit.
- Prepare an expired-listing kit.
- Set monthly goals for listing appointments.
- Send a press release to a newspaper about new affiliation with company (see *5 Minutes to a Great Real Estate Letter* for sample press release).
- Set 3 month goals as a real estate agent for sales and completion of items on list.
- Set 6 month goals for sales and completion of items on list.
- Set 12 month goals for your real estate career.
- Begin reading one book related to real estate to help your career.
- If you are a REALTOR®, set up your account with www.Realtor.org and begin looking at Field Guides regarding topics you have an interest in.
- Have a Web site prepared and coordinate it with the registered URL.

First 6 Weeks in The Real Estate Business

Week 1

> Determine your SOI and place it into computer software database.
> Order necessary business cards and other supplies needed.
> Begin reading a real estate marketing book.
> Begin working on a business plan.
> Begin working on a marketing plan.
> Send out press releases to local papers (see *5 Minutes to a Great Real Estate Letter* for help with this topic).

Week 2

> Finalize SOI list.
> Finish business plan.
> Finish marketing plan.
> Have a broker review both plans with you.
> Begin setting goals (make sure you work with your manager or broker in this area).
> Practice scripts (see www.GoStarPower.com for more help with scripts)!
> Prepare agent resume.
> Prepare company resume.

Week 3

> If cards are in, send them out with letters to your SOI (see letter later in this chapter).
> Begin work on presentations for buyers, sellers, FSBO, and expired listings.
> Continue to study and read articles or real estate books.
> Begin preparing a list of FSBOs and expired listings to contact.

Week 4

> Begin a daily goal sheet to work on contacts and other prospecting issues.
> Put together a neighborhood or area report on housing prices in your marketplace.

Week 5

> Continue to prospect and fine-tune your presentation material.
> Choose a "farm" area or subdivision to work on a regular basis.
> Meet with manager and/or broker to evaluate your performance.

Week 6

> Contact your SOI with a second letter.
> Develop and use your daily goal sheet on a regular basis.
> Send letters to your farm area or subdivision.
> Send "Just Sold" postcards to agent in office.
> Work an open house for an experienced agent in office.
> Develop a working relationship with a local mortgage loan officer.

509 East Main St.
Park Hills, MO 63601
Office: 573-756-0077
Cell: 573-760-4220 Fax: 573-756-1336
Email: John@RealEstateTechGuy.com
Website: www.RealEstateTechGuy.com

We're Not #1, You Are!

[Date]

«Address Block»

«Greeting Line»

I hope all is well with you and your family and the recent days have brought peace and happiness to you all. I know it may come as some surprise that I am in the middle of a new career change. Recently I attended and passed the prelicense real estate school and obtained my real estate license. Yes, I'm now ready to help you with your real estate needs and would count it an honor to do so. As you are aware, real estate is a commission-only business, and therefore my success relies heavily on referrals from you. I have enclosed several cards for you to pass along to anyone you may know who is considering buying or selling real estate.

Again, I hope all is well with you and your family. I appreciate your time and hope we can visit personally soon. Thank you in advance for any referrals you can send my way.

Sincerely,

[Agent's Name]
[Agent's Title]

509 East Main St.
Park Hills, MO 63601
Office: 573-756-0077
Cell: 573-760-4220 Fax: 573-756-1336
Email: John@RealEstateTechGuy.com
Website: www.RealEstateTechGuy.com

We're Not #1, You Are!

[Date]

«Address Block»

«Greeting Line»

Yes, I've finally done it! I've finally completed and passed the real estate prelicense schooling and passed the exam and officially made my new career change! I'm excited about my affiliation with *[company name]* and the education and marketing opportunities they provide to their real estate clients. If you're in the market for buying or selling real estate, I would love to help you. You might also know of someone who may need my services; if so, please pass along one of the enclosed business cards to them. Referrals are a big part of my business, and I would appreciate your remembering me if you know of someone in the market to buy or sell.

I hope all is well with you and your family, and I hope that we can talk on the phone or visit in person soon so that I can share more with you about my new career. Thanks so much for your time, and I hope to hear from you soon.

Sincerely,

[Agent's Name]
[Agent's Title]

509 East Main St.
Park Hills, MO 63601
Office: 573-756-0077
Cell: 573-760-4220 Fax: 573-756-1336
Email: John@RealEstateTechGuy.com
Website: www.RealEstateTechGuy.com

We're Not #1, You Are!

[Date]

«Address Block»

«Greeting Line»

Believe it or not, I am now officially a real estate agent for *[company name]*! Yes, after weeks of preparing for the real estate examination, I have passed the test and I am now ready to help you and consumers with your real estate needs. As you are aware, real estate agents rely heavily on referrals from friends. Therefore, please keep me in mind if you know of someone who might be interested in buying or selling a home. I would love to have the opportunity to work with you or your friends on any real estate needs and would count it an honor to do so.

As always, I appreciate your friendship and I want to thank you in advance for any referrals you can send my way. I hope to hear from you soon.

Sincerely,

[Agent's Name]
[Agent's Title]

509 East Main St.
Park Hills, MO 63601
Office: 573-756-0077
Cell: 573-760-4220 Fax: 573-756-1336
Email: John@RealEstateTechGuy.com
Website: www.RealEstateTechGuy.com

We're Not #1, You Are!

[Date]

«Address Block»

«Greeting Line»

You've trusted me for many years as a friend, and now you and your friends can trust me with your real estate needs. Yes, it's official, I'm now affiliated with *[company name]* and can help you with your real estate needs. If you're in the market to buy or sell a home or if you know of someone who needs real estate services, please think of me. Referrals are an important part of my success as a real estate professional.

I do appreciate your friendship *(friend's name), a*nd I hope you will remember me the next time you hear of someone needing to buy or sell real estate. I've enclosed several business cards for you to have for future reference.

Thank you for your time, and I hope to hear from you soon.

Sincerely,

[Agent's Name]
[Agent's Title]

509 East Main St.
Park Hills, MO 63601
Office: 573-756-0077
Cell: 573-760-4220 Fax: 573-756-1336
Email: John@RealEstateTechGuy.com
Website: www.RealEstateTechGuy.com

We're Not #1, You Are!

[Date]

«Address Block»

«Greeting Line»

I realize this letter may come as a surprise and shock to you, but yes, I'm now selling real estate as a full-time career for *[company name]*. After years of work with my previous employment, I thought that it was time to make a career change to a profession I have always had an interest in. After preparing for several weeks through real estate schooling and passing the state exam, I am now ready to help you with your real estate needs. I also ask that you keep my name available for anyone interested in buying or selling real estate and that you mention my name as a possible source for them to go to for help for their buying and selling. I would count it an honor to assist you and your friends with your real estate needs.

As always, thank you for your friendship and for any referrals you can send my way. Feel free to call anytime if you have any questions about the local real estate economy.

Sincerely,

[Agent's Name]
[Agent's Title]

The following pages show some possible letters an experienced agent might consider using to contact their SOI and to jump-start their real estate career.

509 East Main St.
Park Hills, MO 63601
Office: 573-756-0077
Cell: 573-760-4220 Fax: 573-756-1336
Email: John@RealEstateTechGuy.com
Website: www.RealEstateTechGuy.com

We're Not #1, You Are!

[Date]

«Address Block»

«Greeting Line»

After 20 years of serving the *[area]* area's real estate needs for many buyers and sellers, I have come to note that customer service and thoroughness on each and every deal is imperative. I have taken pride in trying to provide this type of real estate professionalism for my real estate clients over the years.

I also understand how important customers like you are for my real estate business to grow and prosper. Without your referrals and word of mouth from others I would not be where I am today.

As always, thank you for your business and support, and I hope that you will continue to refer others to me through the years for any real estate needs they may have. Thank you so much for your time and for your friendship.

Sincerely,

[Agent's Name]
[Agent's Title]

509 East Main St.
Park Hills, MO 63601
Office: 573-756-0077
Cell: 573-760-4220 Fax: 573-756-1336
Email: John@RealEstateTechGuy.com
Website: www.RealEstateTechGuy.com

We're Not #1, You Are!

[Date]

«Address Block»

«Greeting Line»

After *[XXX]* number of years in the real estate business, I have decided that it is time for a change. Yes, I now have a new logo and slogan for my real estate business. Enclosed you will find a new business card that shows this image and my new logo *[slogan and or statement here]*.

As always, your referrals are a vital part for the success of my real estate business. Thank you so much for referring your friends and others who are interested in buying or selling real estate to me.

Your business is greatly appreciated.

Sincerely,

[Agent's Name]
[Agent's Title]

509 East Main St.
Park Hills, MO 63601
Office: 573-756-0077
Cell: 573-760-4220 Fax: 573-756-1336
Email: John@RealEstateTechGuy.com
Website: www.RealEstateTechGuy.com

We're Not #1, You Are!

[Date]

«Address Block»

«Greeting Line»

One of my goals and missions for this year was to develop a new slogan and vision statement for my real estate business. After months of research, review, and self-analysis, I have decided that *[company slogan]* best describes my real estate business. I have enclosed a new business card with my logo and slogan, and I hope that you will continue to remember me for any real estate needs you may have. Without your referrals and support, it would be difficult for me to continue to do as well as I do with my real estate career.

As always, thank you for your support and referring others to me with their real estate needs.

Sincerely,

[Agent's Name]
[Agent's Title]

509 East Main St.
Park Hills, MO 63601
Office: 573-756-0077
Cell: 573-760-4220 Fax: 573-756-1336
Email: John@RealEstateTechGuy.com
Website: www.RealEstateTechGuy.com

We're Not #1, You Are!

[Date]

«Address Block»

«Greeting Line»

It is hard to believe I have been practicing real estate for *[XXX]* years, and, to be quite honest with you, my longevity and continued success in the real estate business would not be possible without the help from people like you. Referrals and recommendations from you and others I know are essential for my career.

This letter is just to say thank you for your business and support and to remind you to refer me when anyone you know needs help with real estate needs. I do appreciate your friendship and your time.

Sincerely,

[Agent's Name]
[Agent's Title]

509 East Main St.
Park Hills, MO 63601
Office: 573-756-0077
Cell: 573-760-4220 Fax: 573-756-1336
Email: John@RealEstateTechGuy.com
Website: www.RealEstateTechGuy.com

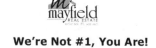

We're Not #1, You Are!

[Date]

«Address Block»

«Greeting Line»

When it comes to selecting a real estate agent with experience, trust and knowledge are a few of the important features that most consumers look for. As you might know, This is awkward phrasing–how about: "As you might know, this is my number of years *[XXX]* in the real estate business, and I am proud to have helped many people over my real estate tenure in buying and selling real estate. If you know of someone who may be interested in any real estate needs, please remember me and suggest to your friends to give me a call. I would love to help them and promise to give the best service possible. Your support and referrals are an important part of my success as a real estate professional.

Thank you in advance for your referrals, and please feel free to call me any time you have any questions.

Sincerely,

[Agent's Name]
[Agent's Title]

509 East Main St.
Park Hills, MO 63601
Office: 573-756-0077
Cell: 573-760-4220 Fax: 573-756-1336
Email: John@RealEstateTechGuy.com
Website: www.RealEstateTechGuy.com

We're Not #1, You Are!

[Date]

«Address Block»

«Greeting Line»

Experience counts! As a real estate professional I have come to know that when it comes to buying or selling real estate, experience does count. From the listing details to the title and escrow responsibilities, having an experienced real estate agent who can assist you with all of these details is important. This is my number of years *[XXX]* in real estate business, and I am proud to be a part of the small percentage of agents who are still in the business and who can still promote their experience as an aid in helping buyers and sellers with their real estate needs. If you are thinking about buying or selling, or know of someone who is, please keep me in mind.

You can reach me at *[agent's phone number]* or visit my Web site *[agent's Web site]*.

As always, thank you for your time and friendship and, most importantly, for any future referrals you happen to send my way.

Sincerely,

[Agent's Name]
[Agent's Title]

Top Ten Things Most Experienced Real Estate Agents Can Help You With

1. **Negotiating.** Although negotiation is something that can be taught, there is only one real means of mastering the negotiation skills and that is through experience. As an experienced real estate agent, I have been in many negotiating situations and circumstances and I believe this experience can help you with your real estate needs.

2. **Understanding and knowing consumer.** For someone new to the real estate business and especially sales, the inability to read or understand what the consumer may be objecting to can possibly stop the closing of the sale. For the real estate professional, experience in understanding and reading human behavior and personality styles is an asset to have on your team and to help expedite the selling process.

3. **Repeat business.** Unfortunately, new real estate agents do not have their cliental or consumer database built up for customers they have worked with in the past. The experienced real estate agent generally has many contacts and leads with whom he or she has worked over the years who can guide and direct the real estate agent in the right direction.

4. **Knowing the market.** Experienced real estate agents tend to have a better feel for know the market what prices properties should bring, and, for a buyer, if they are setting too high a price.

5. **Helping to avoid legal pitfalls.** Unfortunately, many new agents have not had the experience or expertise to negotiate a lot of real estate deals. An experienced agent will know how to structure a counter-offer when dual contracts come in.

6. **Experienced agents have more contacts with vendors and other people who will be working on your behalf during the closing process.** A good experienced agent who has been around for several years has probably built up a good rapport with a local title company and the buyers themselves. If an appraisal needs a rush or a title commitment has a problem that needs to be corrected, experienced agents know whom to go to and how to help get these problems resolved very quickly with very few headaches.

7. **Experienced agents have usually come across certain situations and/or problems before and are familiar with how to solve such problems.** You can always draw from the experienced agent's years of service to help you with your real estate transaction and the difficulties that may arise.

8. **Stability!** Most experienced agents have a stability that you can count on while your property is listed.

9. **Marketing power.** An experienced agent will normally have the marketing power and database of clients and customers to help promote your property. Relying on someone who knows where and how to market your real estate is essential for positive results.

10. **Proven track record!** Most experienced agents have a proven track record that shows, when it comes to selling real estate, they can get the job done!

Promises I'll fulfil for You When I Market Your Property

1. Communicate. I promise to stay in touch and communicate regularly.
2. Care. I will use due care when completing the listing agreement and all necessary paperwork.
3. Obedience. I will be obedient to all of your requests provided they fall within the real estate license law.
4. Accounting. I promise to account for all of your valuables, such as keys, surveys, seasonal photographs, etc.
5. Loyalty. I will be loyal to you throughout the real estate transaction and promise not to discuss any information with agents or others.
6. Disclosure. I promise to disclose any and all material facts I learn through the transaction.
7. Put your property in Multiple Listing Service (MLS).
8. Prepare good advertising copy. I will write attractive, eye-catching copy for all newspapers and MLS remarks. If you need assistance with advertising or MLS copy for your listings, see my book *5 Minutes to a Great Real Estate Ad,* published by Thomson Learning. You'll find hundreds of catchy advertising remarks to use with your daily real estate business.
9. Take good digital photos for the MLS.
10. Verify and check all information in the MLS for accuracy.
11. Send you copies of how your home appears in the MLS.
12. Send you copies of how your home appears on our company Web site.
13. Place a for-sale sign on the property.
14. Place a flyer box next to the for-sale sign on your property.
15. Send flyers to the top 20 agents in our real estate board within the first 20 days of the listing.
16. Report to you on a regular basis about the marketing activity.
17. Place a lock box on the property (if requested).
18. Make sure your property is advertised on a regular basis through our company and my own marketing efforts.
19. Hold an agent open house, if agreeable to you, for the local real estate community to tour.
20. Hold a public open house, if agreeable to you.
21. Update photos on a regular basis.

22. Provide a minimum of one report every 2 weeks on how the marketing efforts are coming along for your property.
23. Keep you posted on what properties are selling for in our marketplace on a regular basis.
24. Send postcards to neighborhood about your property for sale.
25. Send postcards about open house.
26. Send postcards about price reductions if this is a route we explore.
27. Send postcards and flyers to other agents if the price is reduced.
28. Prepare a home-marketing book with disclosures and other information about your property available when others preview your home.

Another important marketing tool to use as a real estate professional is stationery for all of your correspondence. With HP Real Estate Marketing Assistant (REMA) software, you can develop your own stationery and envelopes to use in your real estate business. There are hundreds of themes to choose from with the software and making a consistent theme with all of your reports, postcards, stationery, and envelopes can help build your brand and image in your marketplace. The following pages show some examples of how you can use a theme to promote your image across several types of correspondence. Note that both examples are taken from *5 Minutes to a Great Real Estate Letter*, published by Thomson Learning. Note that the following fax template is one of many found on the CD-ROM from *5 Minutes to a Great Real Estate Letter*.

509 East Main St.
Park Hills, MO 63601
Office: 573-756-0077
Cell: 573-760-4220 Fax: 573-756-1336
Email: John@RealEstateTechGuy.com
Website: www.RealEstateTechGuy.com

We're Not #1, You Are!

[Date]

«Address Block»

«Greeting Line»

Hi, my name is *[agent's name]*, and I noticed your listing recently expired from our Multiple Listing Service (MLS). Unfortunately, this means that your property does not appear in any computer searches other real estate agents use when working with potential buyers in your price range.

If you're still interested in selling your property, I would love to visit with you and explain some of my marketing ideas that have been successful for many of my clients. I have enclosed a sample flyer and a postcard that I use in my marketing campaigns for new listings.

If I can help in any way, please give me a call. I hope to hear from you soon.

Yours Sincerely,

[Agent's Name]

509 East Main St.
Park Hills, MO 63601
Office: 573-756-0077
Cell: 573-760-4220 Fax: 573-756-1336
Email: John@RealEstateTechGuy.com
Website: www.RealEstateTechGuy.com

We're Not #1, You Are!

[Date]

«Address Block»

«Greeting Line»

Fax

To: *[Click here and type name]*   **Fax:** *[Click here and type fax number]*
From: *[Agent's name]*   **Date:** *[e.g., September 28, 2007]*
CC: *[Click here and type name]*   **Pages:** *[Type # of page, including cover]*
Re: *[Click here and type subject of fax]*

☐ Urgent   ☐ For Review   ☐ Please Comment   ☐ Please Reply   ☐ Please Recycle

The following facsimile contains the documents you requested for the property you're appraising at *[property address]*. Please let me know if there is anything else that you need to complete this appraisal. For your information, I have included some important dates we must meet to remain in compliance with this transaction.

Date for closing _____

Date appraisal needed _____

Contact name and phone number for this file _____

As always, thank you for your prompt and professional attention.

Yours truly,

[Agent's Name]
[Agent's Title]

Summary

Agent promotion is important to help distinguish yourself from the competition. There are many ways to help promote yourself as a real estate professional to consumers and clients. Remember that you're a product! Not only do you have to market houses you're selling, but you need to market yourself, too! Try creating a brand, logo, or image based on something you have a passion for. Draw from past experiences or a previous employment to promote your logo or image. Don't forget that consumers will normally recognize you as the agent for real estate in the marketplace if you do a good job keeping your name and brand out in front of them on a regular basis.

Finally, use stationery and matching envelopes for all of your marketing needs. Tie in your *free* reports with the same stationery, and if you have a logo or slogan, incorporate it on all of your materials also. By following a few simple rules you should notice a big increase in your name recognition as the agent to do business with for real estate in your hometown.

9 Online Marketing Ideas

In my book, *5 Minutes to Maximizing Real Estate Technology*, I discuss several of the new and exciting technological online marketing products and tools available today. As technology continues to expand and develop, the real estate professional must be ready to embrace the new changes and move forward. As of this writing, innovations such as the following, among many others, are being utilized in the real estate industry:

- Blogging
- Podcasting
- Video podcasts
- Squidoos
- MySpace
- Facebook

Social networking via the internet is a new and upcoming way to communicate, and if you're not able to adapt and adjust to this new type of marketing, you're sure to miss out on the new generation of business.

Blog Content

Blogging, which has been around for some time now, is still a popular type of online marketing and communication with many real estate agents. Blogging, which stands for "web" and "log," provides the real estate agent with an opportunity to help consumers with educational and specific local community needs. In my book, *5 Minutes to Maximizing Real Estate Technology,* I devote an entire chapter to new and exciting online marketing ideas such as blogging, podcasting, mashups, and more. One way to find out about blogs and some of today's technology advances is to preview and read other real-estate-related technology blog sites. Here are a few Web sites that offer blogs to real estate professionals that may help you get a few new ideas on technology and online marketing.

Real Estate Blogs

http://blog.sellsiusrealestate.com/
http://realestatebusinesssuccess.com/blog/
http://www.bloodhoundrealty.com/BloodhoundBlog/
http://realestatetomato.typepad.com/
http://activerain.com/
http://www.therealtybutler.com/
http://www.raincityguide.com/
http://www.transparentre.com/
http://realestatevoices.com/

You can also do a Google search for "real estate blogs" and find many more sites to view and look for new and exciting ideas in real estate blogs.

What are some items to put on your blog? Basically blogging can be about anything that pertains to consumers who want to buy or sell a home, or to get more information about your local community and/or events taking place in your community. For example, suppose that you're in a marketplace where your community offers various functions and community-related activities throughout the summer or year. You could consider writing a blog to post information about the activities so that consumers can easily find this information. Of course, you can do this on your Web site without a blog, but using a blog and allowing consumers the ability to add comments or thoughts is a new trend and can drive more traffic to your site. A word of caution to the real estate professional who wants to add blogs for participation—be sure to monitor your blogs to stop obscene material from being uploaded to your site. One individual from Springfield, MO, has been using blogs and podcasting for sometime with excellent results—Paul Dizmang discusses how one of his customers set up a blog while looking at homes in their area.

I had a client who we sold a home to a couple of months ago. We only showed him two houses. He took the listings we gave him and he created his own blog site. He would post his comments and I could go in and post my comments and we were able to communicate about what he and his wife wanted via his own personal blog. It was convenient for them and great for us. We knew what he was thinking about every house and through this we were able to find them the right home with only two showings.

The following illustration shows Paul Dizmang's blog he hosts for consumers who need more help with their real estate needs.

The following are some blogs from real estate professionals and their Web sites—you can discover and see how other agents are using blogs to generate more business from online marketing.

Podcasting and Videocasting

Another source of online marketing is through podcasting or videocasting. As new equipment and devices continue to be integrated for today's technology, the use of digital video and other streaming media will continue to grow in popularity. Consumers can now readily access digital and other sources via cellular phones and at home with high-speed Internet connections.

Many real estate professionals are starting to utilize services such as YouTube to promote and advertise their services and listings for sale. Google is also involved in this new Internet offering of videos. With videocasting and/or podcasting you can help consumers with buying and selling real estate, properties for sale, and offer information about yourself and company.

Paul Dizmang, mentioned earlier in the chapter, also uses video podcasting to provide information to his clients. You can normally find Paul doing some clever, off-the-wall mini-videos about real estate and tips and suggestions to avoid when buying or selling a home. In fact, do a search on YouTube™ for "The Hot Tub Realtor," and you'll find Paul sitting in his hot tub, giving consumers advice on the value of what a hot tub offers when you go to buy or sell a home.

The real estate professional must keep in mind that, with services such as blogging, podcasting, and videocasting, it will require time for this to be successful. Setting up and maintaining a blog or podcast is a challenge and can take up a lot of valuable time that could be spent prospecting for listings. However, it does provide the real estate agent the conduit for new ideas and fresh marketing work to break up the same old day in and day out work.

MySpace

MySpace is another new form of online marketing that many younger real estate agents are finding beneficial. MySpace provides content for social networking that is growing in popularity on the World Wide Web along with social networks such as Facebook and Squidoo. In some common areas with MySpace, you can provide links and information to consumers to help with buying or selling a home, as well as create a group of contacts with whom you can communicate immediately about new listings, price reductions, and open houses as they become available. To find out more about how MySpace is being utilized by real estate agents, visit www.MySpace.com and search the words "real estate." You should find a wide variety of agents and sites to visit and learn more on how real estate agents are doing business within this new medium.

Squidoo is another new social network that is providing consumers access to individuals who are experts in a particular field of study or topic. With Squidoo, the user develops what is termed a lens in a particular subject matter. For example, a Squidoo member who is a real estate professional, you could develop a lens to buy and sell foreclosed property. Your lens could then have information and access to links, articles, and other sources in this field of study.

Another popular online marketing tool real estate agents are using is Craigslist. Craigslist allows real estate professionals to post properties for sale and rent with detailed descriptions, photos, and links to the property being offered.

Your Web site can be an excellent place for marketing properties and providing information about yourself to consumers surfing the World Wide Web. Your Web site is also a great opportunity for providing "FREE" reports and other downloadable information. You can also use digital videos, blogging, podcasting, and other new online marketing ideas discussed in conjunction with your Web site and other online activities.

Regardless of which online marketing ideas you choose, it's important to remember to promote your Web site, podcast, blog, or Squidoo through all of your marketing and advertisement ideas. The following shows a sample postcard you might consider using to promote your blog, podcast, or Squidoo.

A Little Bit of Everything...

You'll find a little bit of everything on my real estate blog. Check it out at www.RealEstateTechGuy.com

For all of your real estate needs, call John Mayfield at 573-431-XXXX

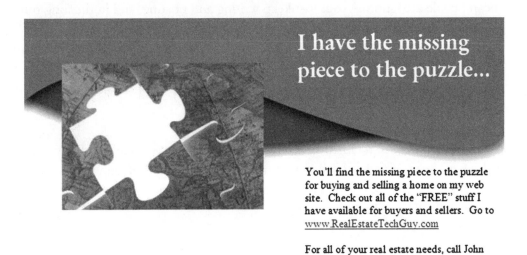

John Mayfield GRI, CRB, ABR

PRSRT STD U.S.
POSTAGE PAID
CITY, STATE
YOUR PERMIT NO.

509 East Main St.
Park Hills, MO 63601
Office: 573-756-0077
Fax: 573-756-1336
Cell: 573-760-4220
Email:
John@RealEstateTechGuy.com
Website:
www.RealEstateTechGuy.com

Need a Buyer's Agent?

«FirstName» «LastName»
«Address1» «Address2»
«City» «State» «PostalCode»

I have the missing piece to the puzzle...

You'll find the missing piece to the puzzle for buying and selling a home on my web site. Check out all of the "FREE" stuff I have available for buyers and sellers. Go to www.RealEstateTechGuy.com

For all of your real estate needs, call John Mayfield at 573-431-XXXX

Things to Remember With Blogging

1. **Stay on top of local community events.** Use your blog to promote and encourage readers to support the local activities.
2. **Keep abreast of local newsworthy items.** Keep in mind that blogging can become controversial, and you want to stay away from editorializing a news item or taking a particular side. Rather, use the blog to help provide information for the reader and try to remain neutral on sensitive items.

3. **Read other local, state, and national news items.**   Provide links for readers when you can.

4. **Show other blogs.**

5. **Provide links of interest or value to the readers.**   A good example might be helping the reader find information on foreclosed homes, tax tips, questions and answers for home buyers, etc.

6. **Set a goal on your calendar of dates to post your blog.**   Although blogging can be fun and should be done at your convenience, having dates, goals, and scheduling when to upload and change your blog is important.

7. **Keep a folder on your desktop of interesting ideas and topics you would like to write about.**   Don't worry about writing a blog then; just keep a running list of ideas and topics to refer to later.

8. **Keep your blogs short and to the point.**   No one likes to read when someone rambles with nothing to say. State your point, provide information or a link, and you'll have many people come back to read your blog on a daily basis.

9. **Don't expect people to reply or respond to every blog post.**   Sometimes you may go weeks without having a posted response on your blog, but this does not mean people are ignoring you. Just keep writing and posting, and in the long run you're sure to profit from your blog.

10. **Read other blogs to get new ideas on how and what you should write about.**   Reading other blogs is a good way to gain insight into how the field of blogging works, but always give another blogger credit when you quote or use an idea from their blog.

In my book *5 Minutes to Maximizing Real Estate Technology*, published by Thomson Learning, I have a section and a detailed system for setting up and utilizing a podcast on an annual basis. You can purchase this book from any local bookstore, Amazon, or from my Web site at www.RealEstateTechGuy.com.

Summary

In closing, remember that online marketing can be effective and save you time and money if implemented correctly. If you plan to incorporate any of the ideas listed in this chapter, remember that you need to find a niche or topic that interests you, promote it heavily, and remain consistent! Find ways to utilize your new online marketing ideas to promote yourself as the real estate expert, and always remember that, to be effective and gain support and respect from the reader, something of value should be exchanged. By providing good-quality content on a regular basis, you will achieve this goal and be well on your way to making money using today's new online marketing mediums.

Finally, don't forget to check out my book, *5 Minutes to Maximizing Real Estate Technology*, for more online marketing ideas and help.

10 Brokerage Marketing Plan

$\mathbf{M}$any real estate brokers are faced with the challenges of making sure their advertising and marketing functions operate smoothly. Today, the broker's main aim is to see that the real estate agents in the office help build and maintain a consistent brand and image. Guidelines and rules need to be set in place to ensure the office image is delivered without any change in all of the various marketing efforts by the company and the licensees. Since discussing these issues and concerns could form an entire book in itself, we'll focus our attention in this chapter on how the broker can advertise or market to other real estate licensees in hopes of getting that agent to come to work for them. The letters and postcards shown throughout this chapter can be used to help encourage or recruit agents to the firm.

The following pages show sample letters a broker could incorporate into a recruiting plan for new or existing agents. The sample letters will be followed by a few postcard examples to implement for a drip marketing program, sample e-mail notes, and a sample form on why your company should be considered for their real estate career.

509 East Main St.
Park Hills, MO 63601
Office: 573-756-0077
Cell: 573-760-4220 Fax: 573-756-1336
Email: John@RealEstateTechGuy.com
Website: www.RealEstateTechGuy.com

We're Not #1, You Are!

[Date]

«Address Block»

«Greeting Line»

I hope that things are going well for you and your real estate career. I wanted to take a small moment of your time to ask you three very important questions:

1. Are you satisfied with your real estate career?
2. Do you feel you're in the right position for your real estate career to grow over the next 3 to 5 years?
3. Are you utilizing all of the possible resources available to help your real estate career grow?

As the broker/manager of *[company name]*, these are the three important questions that I remind myself of everyday regarding the real estate professionals who are a part of my team. I understand the competitiveness and the need for my team members to not only have a positive growth at the current time with their real estate career but to see them excel and move forward in the future. I am also reminded that, as real estate professionals, they need access to all of the resources available to them to help make their businesses grow.

If you had to answer any of the above questions in a manner that was not how you wished you could answer, maybe we should visit in the near future. For a *free*, confidential, no obligation talk on how *[company name]* can help you in your real estate career, call me at *[company phone number]*.

I appreciate your time, and I look forward to speaking with you soon.

Yours truly,

[Broker's Name]
[Broker's Title]

509 East Main St.
Park Hills, MO 63601
Office: 573-756-0077
Cell: 573-760-4220 Fax: 573-756-1336
Email: John@RealEstateTechGuy.com
Website: www.RealEstateTechGuy.com

We're Not #1, You Are!

[Date]

«Address Block»

«Greeting Line»

I realize that changing real estate offices can be an overwhelming and daunting thought for the real estate professional. However, sometimes change is good. Change does not always reflect the fact that there is a problem or that anything is wrong with the person's productivity and ability to perform. Sometimes change is just needed for a breath of fresh air. If you feel as though your real estate career needs a shot in the arm or turn in a new direction, I would love to visit with you about such a change.

At *[company name]* we're excited about the accomplishments we have seen in the past few years and our growth in the future. I feel that you would be an excellent addition to our team of real estate agents, and I would love to have the opportunity to visit with you and share some of this excitement.

As always, thank you for your time, and I look forward to hearing from you soon.

Yours truly,

[Broker's Name]
[Broker's Title]

Brokerage Marketing Plan   141

509 East Main St.
Park Hills, MO 63601
Office: 573-756-0077
Cell: 573-760-4220 Fax: 573-756-1336
Email: John@RealEstateTechGuy.com
Website: www.RealEstateTechGuy.com

mayfield
REAL ESTATE

We're Not #1, You Are!

[Date]

«Address Block»

«Greeting Line»

The Chinese definition of insanity is *doing the same thing over and over but expecting different results.* Unfortunately, many real estate professionals follow this course of action over the course of their real estate careers when things are not going well. We all want different results, but are we really willing to make the change to accomplish those desired goals?

At *[company name]* our goal and mission is to help our agents and team members achieve their dreams and desires! That is why each year our agents are put through a vigorous goal-planning and dream-listing exercise. Without goals and dreams, it is difficult for the real estate agent to achieve a winning attitude. If you find yourself in that same rut and your real estate career needs a boost or change of direction, I would love to visit with you. Call me, *[broker/branch manager's name]*, at your earliest convenience so we can discuss new ways and possibilities to aim your real estate career in a positive direction. You can reach me at *[broker/branch manager's phone number]* any time. I look forward to your phone call, and I hope you will go out and make today a great day!

Sincerely,

[Broker/Branch Manger's Name]
[Broker/Branch Manger's Title]

509 East Main St.
Park Hills, MO 63601
Office: 573-756-0077
Cell: 573-760-4220 Fax: 573-756-1336
Email: John@RealEstateTechGuy.com
Website: www.RealEstateTechGuy.com

We're Not #1, You Are!

[Date]

«Address Block»

«Greeting Line»

There is a story about an old logging road up in the northern woods of Canada. The sign on the side of the road says this: "Road ruts ahead. Choose carefully which rut you get in as you'll be in it for the next 20 miles."

Many times as real estate professionals when we start our career with an agency or real estate team, we find out early in the game that the road we have traveled is not the one we had desired. Making an office change as a real estate agent can be a big decision and one that many real estate agents choose to ignore or avoid. In reality the choice of staying in the same rut for the next 2 or 3 years or moving yourself to a smoother road where the possibilities and opportunities can become promising should not be that difficult of a decision. At *[company name]* we pride ourselves on helping agents move from those rough and unpleasant real estate roadway experiences to an enjoyable transition of the real estate business. We have an extensive educational and training program for our real estate team players as well as a technology resources center that is unmatched by any organization in town. Our agents have opportunities that many agents only dream about. If you would be interested in learning all of the exciting resources that *[company name]* can provide you, feel *free* to contact me at *[broker's phone number]* so I can discuss this further with you. I appreciate your time. I hope you have a great day, and I look forward to hearing from you.

Sincerely,

[Broker's Name]
[Broker's Title]

This letter would be ideal to use when the time changes in April and August.

509 East Main St.
Park Hills, MO 63601
Office: 573-756-0077
Cell: 573-760-4220 Fax: 573-756-1336
Email: John@RealEstateTechGuy.com
Website: www.RealEstateTechGuy.com

We're Not #1, You Are!

[Date]

«Address Block»

«Greeting Line»

It is time to change your clock. That is right, another time change is soon upon us. If your real estate career is not where you think it should be, perhaps it is time to make a change with your career as well. At *[company name]* we're always looking for new real estate agents to join our progressive and willing real estate team.

If you would be interested in joining one of the fastest growing real estate organizations in the *[city name]* area, call me, *[manager's name]*, for a *free*, private interview on how our organization can improve your real estate business and put time back on your side. Call me, *[branch manager's name]*, at *[branch manger's cell phone number]* so we can discuss these exciting opportunities.

I appreciate your time in reading this letter, and I look forward to hearing from you soon.

Sincerely,

[Broker's Name]
[Broker's Title]

509 East Main St.
Park Hills, MO 63601
Office: 573-756-0077
Cell: 573-760-4220 Fax: 573-756-1336
Email: John@RealEstateTechGuy.com
Website: www.RealEstateTechGuy.com

We're Not #1, You Are!

[Date]

«Address Block»

«Greeting Line»

A new year is upon us, and with a new year comes resolutions, goals, dreams, and an exciting outlook for your real estate career. It is also a great time to consider making a change to an organization that can help you achieve those new goals that you have set out to accomplish. At *[company name]* we pride ourselves on helping real estate agents turn their dreams and goals into realities. Our training and resource tools are unmatched by any other organization in town. If you have big plans for the coming year and your goals are set high, you need to make sure you are with a real estate company that can help you reach that next level. Call me, *[broker's name]*, at *[broker's phone number]* so we can discuss and map out strategies to help you reach your goals for the coming year.

Thank you so much for taking time out to read this letter, and I look forward to hearing from you soon.

Sincerely,

[Broker's Name]
[Broker's Title]

This letter would be ideal to use at the beginning of Spring.

509 East Main St.
Park Hills, MO 63601
Office: 573-756-0077
Cell: 573-760-4220 Fax: 573-756-1336
Email: John@RealEstateTechGuy.com
Website: www.RealEstateTechGuy.com

We're Not #1, You Are!

[Date]

«Address Block»

«Greeting Line»

Are you ready for your real estate career to "spring" forward in a new direction? At *[company name]* we can help your real estate career move to a whole new level. Our real estate team prides itself on giving superior and professional service. We have *[number of agents]* serving the *[area]*. We have the tools and resources that can help take your real estate career to a new level.

If you would like to have a private, no-pressure, no-strings-attached interview, contact me, *[branch manger's name]*, at *[branch manger's phone number]*.

I appreciate you taking time out to read this letter. I look forward to hearing from your soon, and I feel confident that by moving forward with this invitation, you're taking the first steps in "springing" your real estate career to a new level.

Sincerely,

[Broker's Name]
[Broker's Title]

509 East Main St.
Park Hills, MO 63601
Office: 573-756-0077
Cell: 573-760-4220 Fax: 573-756-1336
Email: John@RealEstateTechGuy.com
Website: www.RealEstateTechGuy.com

We're Not #1, You Are!

[Date]

«Address Block»

«Greeting Line»

I have noticed your real estate production from our Multiple Listing Service, and I must admit I am quite impressed by the transactions that you have closed over the past few months. I realize that making a change when productivity is up is not always something most real agents think about, but at the same time I also understand that your transactions might increase further by associating with a progressive and leading company such as ours. We have experienced many new recruits such as yourself who had promising results at other smaller brokerage offices and have doubled and tripled their income by joining our team. I would love to have a few moments of your time to tell you about some of the benefits and resources that we can provide you at *[company name]*. Feel *free* to call me at *[broker's phone number]* at your earliest convenience to discuss some of the exciting tools that are available and waiting for you at *[company name]*.

Again, congratulations on your excellent year, and I look forward to hearing from you soon.

Sincerely,

[Broker's Name]
[Broker's Title]

Brokerage Marketing Plan   147

This letter is ideal to use right after a National Football League Super Bowl event.

509 East Main St.
Park Hills, MO 63601
Office: 573-756-0077
Cell: 573-760-4220 Fax: 573-756-1336
Email: John@RealEstateTechGuy.com
Website: www.RealEstateTechGuy.com

We're Not #1, You Are!

[Date]

«Address Block»

«Greeting Line»

I am sure you recently had an opportunity to hear or watch the Nation Football League's Super Bowl game this past week. As I think about the winning team and the celebration among team members, I am reminded that, for any organization to succeed and win, it requires the right group of people. Whether it is an organization, association, team, or any other collective group of people, to succeed and become number one, you must work together and encourage and support the others you are associated with. At *[company name]* we strive to incorporate that same team spirit that other winning organizations provide. We are committed to encouraging one another, helping and providing the right tools so that our organization can be number one. If joining an exciting and aggressive real estate firm like this is appealing to you, then I encourage you to not hesitate and call me today for a private, no-strings-attached interview. Call me, *[broker's name]*, at *[broker's phone number]* so that we can begin discussing ways for you to become a part of our winning organization.

I appreciate your time in reading this letter, and I look forward to your phone call in the near future.

Sincerely,

[Broker's Name]
[Broker's Title]

Don't let your real estate career go down the wrong road and lead you to no where. Start your career in the right direction with the right company. Find out all the positive benefits of affiliating with *[Company Name]*. Call *[Broker or Manager Name]* at *[Agency Phone Number]* for more information.

Why do so many real estate agents affiliate with *[Company Name]*? Could it be the marketing plans they offer their agents? The technology tools they provide their real estate professionals? The aggressive compensation splits each team member receives or perhaps it's just a great friendly professional environment. Whatever the case you too can experience the same great benefits. For more information to find out how you can become part of the *[Company Name]* team call *[Broker or Manager Name]* at *[Agency Phone Number*

Note: Both post card examples use copy from "5 Minutes to a Great Real Estate Ad," The Brokerage Recruitment Chapter. For more ads check out this book today at *www.5-Minutes.com*.

Better Days

Does your real estate career seem stuck and you don't enjoy going to work everyday? Good news, better day are ahead at *[Company Name]*! We can provide you with excellent compensation splits, a comfortable and professional work environment and the right tools to help your business grow. To find out more information contact *[Broker or Manager Name]* *[Office Location/Area]*

You'll Flip

When you hear all off the great services and benefits we provide our real estate agents on a daily basis. Call *[Broker or Manager Name]* at *[Agency Phone Number]* to schedule a private confidential interview and to receive your free portfolio of all of our special details. Now hiring new and experienced agents for a limited time only. Call quickly before this offer is too late. Call *[Agency Phone Number]*

Note: Both post card examples use copy from "5 Minutes to a Great Real Estate Ad," The Brokerage Recruitment Chapter. For more ads check out this book today at *www.5-Minutes.com*.

Drip E-Mail Marketing Campaign

You can also use the sample recruit ads from *5 Minutes to a Great Real Estate Ad,* The Brokerage Recruitment chapter, as drip e-mail marketing ideas, too. Here's an example of how one of the sample recruitment ads was converted into an e-mail:

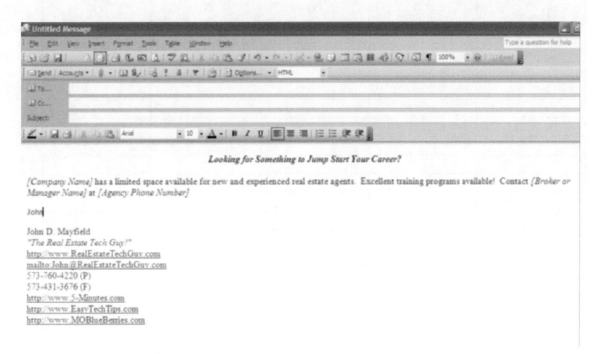

Another good marketing idea is to have a comparison chart prepared regarding your real estate company. The following table is a sample comparison chart you might consider using when recruiting new and experienced agents. Using a visual to compare the opportunities and services you offer agents and those offered by the competition is helpful in winning new sales associates to your team. You will need to take the time to think about some of the services and special features you provide your agents and whether those same services are offered by the competition.

This table is available on the enclosed CD-ROM.

Checklist on "Why Your Company"

Services Offered	[Your Company]	[Company Name]	[Company Name]	[Company Name]
Company Training	*Yes*	*No*	*No*	*Yes*

Summary

As listings are important to the real estate sales agent, prospecting and recruiting for new agents is equally essential to the real estate broker. Make it a point to recruit on a regular basis. You might also consider targeting a few specific real estate agents with letters and postcards found in this chapter. Finally, develop a comparison table on some of the services you offer your agents that the competition does not. Having the ability to show some of the advantages new and experienced agents will have through your office can be the difference maker on whether they choose your office over another.

11 Building a Referral Base

There was an old saying prevalent in my early years as a real estate professional: Work hard the first few years of your career, and then your business will work for you. This is exactly what happened to me as a real estate professional. My first few years as a devoted real estate agent were spent prospecting, working with buyers and sellers, and building my productivity year after year. What happened over these first years of my real estate career is that more and more of my satisfied clients and customers sent more business to me. Many of my buyers and sellers would call to ask for my assistance and to know if I could help them with their next purchase or sale. For some clients, I would handle two or three transactions for them during one calendar year. With that said, it is easy to see that building your referral base from satisfied customers and clients can be a large part of your business. Many of these satisfied customers and clients can and should be placed on your sphere of influence (SOI) list to contact on a regular basis; however, some people you would like to communicate with on a regular basis need not necessarily be on your SOI. Others that need to be contacted on an ongoing basis should be people who come into contact with many new potential buyers and sellers on a daily basis—businesspersons and civic-minded persons. Hospitals, business, chambers of commerce, along with public and private schools, are good sources to communicate with to build a good referral base. The following pages contain some letters, flyers, and other presentation material you might consider delivering individuals, businesses, and organizations. Remember, building a referral base can help generate income of thousands of dollars in your real estate career if worked correctly.

Letter #1 To Human Resource Manager

509 East Main St.
Park Hills, MO 63601
Office: 573-756-0077
Cell: 573-760-4220 Fax: 573-756-1336
Email: John@RealEstateTechGuy.com
Website: www.RealEstateTechGuy.com

We're Not #1, You Are!

[Date]

«*Address Block*»

«*Greeting Line*»

Hello, my name is *[agent's name]*, and I work for *[company's name]* in *[city name]*, and I realize that, as human resource manager for *[company or organization name]*, I'm sure that you come into contact with many new transferees on a regular basis. I have developed a sample Welcome Kit for the *[city name or area]*. This kit includes many important facts and figures about our area and the local real estate economy including statistics on the average sales prices of homes in various areas as well as the days on market it takes for a home to sell. I have gone to great lengths to include school information, employment, and other data that I feel people relocating to our area would find helpful and informative. I am sure that you may have something similar to this that you provide to transferees who are considering your company; however, my kit does place major emphasis on the housing industry in our area. I would love to visit with you at a time in the near future convenient to you to show you my Welcome Kit and to offer to provide these kits at no charge to *[company]* to have available for possible new employees of your organization. Please feel free to call me at your earliest convenience and let me know what would be a good time to go over this new Welcome Kit with you.

I appreciate your time, and I hope to hear from you soon. Please feel free to call me if you have any additional questions.

Yours truly,

[Agent's Name]
[Agent's Title]

Note: To build your own Welcome Kit, visit your local chamber of commerce and begin putting together information about your community. You can and should include the following items in your kit:

Local school information
Community events and other information available from the chamber of commerce
Multiple Listing information on the following:
    Average sales price for area
    Average days on market
    List to sales price ratio
    Various homes currently for sale
Web links to your Web site, board Multiple Listing Web site, and other local Web sites
    with real-estate-related data
Web links to local Web sites for items of interest in community
Parks and recreational activities
Copy of local newspapers
Listing of area religious organizations
Map of city and other local points of interest
Your company resume and information
Your personal resume and information
"FREE" report or reports as included in this book
Moving checklist as included in Chapter 6
Any census data or information appropriate to area, such as jobs, income, and population
    facts and figures
Lenders information for home mortgages
Information on home-related services, such as home inspectors and title insurance
    companies

Be sure and use your personalized stationery as discussed in Chapter 9.

Letter #2 To Human Resource Manager

509 East Main St.
Park Hills, MO 63601
Office: 573-756-0077
Cell: 573-760-4220 Fax: 573-756-1336
Email: John@RealEstateTechGuy.com
Website: www.RealEstateTechGuy.com

We're Not #1, You Are!

[Date]

«Address Block»

«Greeting Line»

Hello, my name is *[agent's name]*, and I work for *[company's name]* in *[city name]*. As a human resource manager for *[company or organization name]*, I understand your need to provide important information to new recruits and employees who may be relocating to our area from around the state and/or country. I would love to assist you in providing your possible transferees with information about our community and especially the local housing market. I have developed a Welcome Kit that assists out-of-town buyers in learning more about the *[local area name]* area. I am making these kits available to your organization "FREE" of charge. If you believe this is something that would help in your recruiting process, please let me know. I would be happy to meet with you and go over the Welcome Kit at a time that is convenient to you.

As always, thank you for your time, and I look forward in meeting with you soon.

Yours truly,

[Agent's Name]
[Agent's Title]

Letter #3 To Human Resource Manager

509 East Main St.
Park Hills, MO 63601
Office: 573-756-0077
Cell: 573-760-4220 Fax: 573-756-1336
Email: John@RealEstateTechGuy.com
Website: www.RealEstateTechGuy.com

We're Not #1, You Are!

[Date]

«*Address Block*»

«*Greeting Line*»

Are you puzzled with questions from new recruits about the local housing market? Do you have all of the answers regarding the average sales price for our area, number of days a home is on the market before selling, and the list to sales price ratio? Do you know what homes typically sell faster in our marketplace? If not, I can help assist you with these answers and many more about our local housing market. As a human resource manager for *[company or organization name]*, I understand your need to provide information to new recruits and employees who may be relocating to our area from around the state and/or country. I have developed a Welcome Kit that assists out-of-town buyers in learning more about the *[local area name]* area. I am making these kits available to your organization "FREE" of charge. If you believe this is something that would help in your recruiting process, please let me know. I would be happy to meet with you and go over the Welcome Kit at a time that is convenient to you.

As always, thank you for your time, and I look forward to meeting with you soon.

Yours truly,

[Agent's Name]
[Agent's Title]

Letter #1 to Local Bank or Area Businessperson

509 East Main St.
Park Hills, MO 63601
Office: 573-756-0077
Cell: 573-760-4220 Fax: 573-756-1336
Email: John@RealEstateTechGuy.com
Website: www.RealEstateTechGuy.com

We're Not #1, You Are!

[Date]

«Address Block»

«Greeting Line»

I hope all is well with your business and that the local economy has been profitable for you. I realize that you know a lot of people offering many different services in our area and that many individuals such as myself consider your referrals a major boon for our businesses. I wanted to take time out to say thank you for all of your support with my real estate career. Without your referrals, my business would not be where it is today. Thank you!

Please know that I am always sending business your way, and let me know if there is ever anything I can do to assist you. I hope you're having a great day!

Yours truly,

[Agent's Name]
[Agent's Title]

Letter #2 to Local Bank or Area Businessperson

509 East Main St.
Park Hills, MO 63601
Office: 573-756-0077
Cell: 573-760-4220 Fax: 573-756-1336
Email: John@RealEstateTechGuy.com
Website: www.RealEstateTechGuy.com

We're Not #1, You Are!

[Date]

«*Address Block*»

«*Greeting Line*»

I have great news to share with you about a new project I have recently completed. I have developed a Welcome Kit that assists out-of-towners in learning more about the *[local area name]* area. I am making these kits available to local organizations "FREE" of charge to share with people they may know who are relocating to our area. If you know of someone who may be moving to the *[local area name]* area, please let me know and I will be glad to forward one to them. I would also be happy to provide you with a Welcome Kit to look over and review. Let me know if this is something you may want, and I will personally bring you one.

As always, thank you for your friendship and support with my real estate careers, and remember to make my new Welcome Kit available to individuals you may know who are considering a move to our area.

Yours truly,

[Agent's Name]
[Agent's Title]

Building a Referral Base   159

Letter #3 to Local Bank or Area Businessperson

509 East Main St.
Park Hills, MO 63601
Office: 573-756-0077
Cell: 573-760-4220 Fax: 573-756-1336
Email: John@RealEstateTechGuy.com
Website: www.RealEstateTechGuy.com

We're Not #1, You Are!

[Date]

«Address Block»

«Greeting Line»

I realize that from time to time you may hear of someone relocating to our area from outside *[name of area]*, and I wanted to make you aware of a new Welcome Kit I recently created. My Welcome Kit assists out-of-town buyers in learning more about the *[local area name]* area and specifically about the local housing economy. The kits are "FREE," and I can mail them directly to your contacts or provide them to you for mailing, whichever is easier for you.

As always, I appreciate your support and help in making my real estate career, and please remember that referrals are an integral part of my success as a real estate professional. Thanks for your time, and I hope to hear from you soon.

Yours truly,

[Agent's Name]
[Agent's Title]

Welcome!

Does your company or organization have a Welcome Kit containing pertinent facts about the local housing market? If not, call me *[agent name]* for a "FREE" copy of my Welcome Kit designed specifically for new families moving into our area.

Call John Mayfield for more information: 573-431-XXXX
www.RealEstateTechGuy.com

The previous illustration shows a sample postcard that you could send to area businesses or human resource managers in your area. The following paragraphs contain material that you could incorporate within other postcards to send over an extended period of time when prospecting for new business.

Sample Postcard Copy

Questions?

Does your potential recruit have questions about the local housing market? If so, I have good news. I've just developed a Welcome Kit providing out-of-town consumers with information about home prices, days on market, and more on our local economy. Call me, *[agent name]*, to receive a copy of this Welcome Kit and to show you how your new relocating families can learn more about our local housing market.

Before They Sign on the Dotted Line

Many potential job transferees won't make a decision to commit to your organization until they know something about the local housing market. If your new recruits have questions about the local housing market, I can help! Call me, *[agent name]*, for a "FREE" copy of my Welcome Kit. My Welcome Kit contains information about our local area and the housing market for *[area name]*. It has a wealth of information for your new employees, and, best of all, it's "FREE!"

Look Professional

If you're interviewing new candidates for potential job positions who are considering relocating to our area, you need to look your best and be able to answer as many questions as possible. That's why I've created a Welcome Kit to help consumers considering a move to our area. My Welcome Kit contains information about our local area and the housing market for *[area name]*. It has a wealth of information for your new employees, and, best of all, it's "FREE!" Call me, *[agent name]*, at *[agent phone number]* to learn how your organization can receive these kits at no charge or obligation.

Summary

Prospecting local businesses, hospitals, schools, and directors of human resources for companies and organizations are excellent ways to build potential business as a real estate professional. Developing and Distributing a Welcome Kit that provides information about the local economy, housing market, recreational activities, schools, and more can help put you in front of many new transferees who are considering relocating to your area and can help build your referral base for life.

12 Summary and Conclusion

In my closing thoughts and statements for *5 Minutes to Great Real Estate Marketing Ideas,* I want to say thank you for your business and support. As with all of my 5 Minutes books, my primary goal is to help agents save time and make more money. As a real estate agent, I understand how difficult it can be to make a full-time living selling real estate. I also know how time can be a factor and how attempting to set up action plans and systems to carry out the needed tasks can be difficult to do. Much of the material I would find as a real estate agent did not have the "professional" feel that I wanted to convey to my clients. I've always wanted to make my letters and presentation materials look professional and to help set me a part from the competition. I believe that with *5 Minutes to a Great Real Estate Letter* I was able to achieve this goal, based on feedback from the agents I have met around the country who have purchased it and used it on a daily basis. This is the greatest compliment any author can have, and I believe this new book, *5 Minutes to Great Real Estate Marketing Ideas,* will achieve the same results. I have researched and studied many materials to implement into the text and tried to maximize ways to make the material in this book easy to use on a regular basis. By engaging the action plans and systems found throughout this book, you should be on your way to developing prospecting campaigns for new clients and maintaining existing relationships through the letters, postcards, and other materials found in this manual. If you have not had a chance to check out the CD-ROM, remember that most of the documents are included on this disk along with videos to help show you how to get the most out of the book and all of the material included with it. You can also visit my Web site at www.RealEstateTechGuy.com for more information.

I love the story that my mother tells about the gentleman who had a hot dog stand. This older fellow owned and operated a small hot dog stand along the highway. He had many billboards and lots of various advertising mechanisms to promote his hot dog stand. People crowded around his hot dog stand everyday to purchase hot dogs from him, and his business flourished and thrived. His younger son decided it was time to go away to college to study business. While away at school the boy learned a lot about the economy and the condition of the country. Arriving home on his first trip back from college, he told his dad that he had learned the country was in the middle of a big depression. Times are tough, the young boy told his father. Don't you think you should cut back on your advertising and marketing ideas? Our country is in bad shape, voiced the lad. His dad thought about these statements and agreed with his son that he was probably doing too much marketing with the state of the economy. After all, my son has been away to school and is educated and knows the pulse and beat of our country's situation, he thought. So the father took down his billboards and stopped his advertising in the local papers. It didn't take too long for his customer base to reduce and for sales to dwindle to nothing. After a few months the father was forced to shut his hot dog stand down. As he locked the door and left his hot dog stand for the last time, he thought, my son was right, we are in the middle of a big depression.

Regardless of your situation or your length of time in the real estate business, remember that advertising is essential and needed at "all" times if you want to succeed and have business. I trust that this book has given you new ideas and ways to promote your business. After all, you're now only 5 minutes away from some GREAT real estate marketing ideas!

Appendix

The following pages show some various examples of flyers, postcards, and other information prepared using HP Real Estate Marketing Assistant Software. Some information has been left blank to show the reader how adding text and photos are all that is needed to construct the marketing materials. Please refer to the enclosed CD-ROM for specific details and for a video on how these materials are produced.

Type Title Here

Type Subtitle Here

John Mayfield GRI, CRB, ABR
509 East Main St.
Park Hills, MO 63601

Features

- Type Text Here
-
-
-
-

Type Text Here

REALTOR

Office: 573-756-0077
Fax: 573-756-1336
Cell: 573-760-4220
Email:
John@RealEstateTechGuy.com
Website:
www.RealEstateTechGuy.com

- Type Text Here
-
-
-

EQUAL HOUSING OPPORTUNITY

mayfield REAL ESTATE
we're not #1, you are!

Type Text Here

Double click here
to insert picture
(suggestion: outside view;
for example panoramic view)

John Mayfield GRI, CRB, ABR

509 East Main St.
Park Hills, MO 63601
Office: 573-756-0077
Cell: 573-760-4220
Fax: 573-756-1336
Email: John@RealEstateTechGuy.com
Website: www.RealEstateTechGuy.com

xt Here

«FirstName» «LastName»
«Address1» «Address2»
«City» «State» «PostalCode»

JUST LISTED – LIVING ON THE LAKE

Handcrafted woodwork is found throughout this *[# Bedrooms]* bedroom and *[# Baths]* bath *[Style of Home]* home. Extra features included are *[Feature 1]*, *[Feature 2]*, and *[Feature 3]*. Call *[Listing Agent]* at *[Phone Number]* for more information. *[Listing Code Number]*.

John and Kerry Mayfield
1450 Hwy. OO
Farmington, MO 63640

John and Kerry Mayfield
1450 Hwy. OO
Farmington, MO 63640

John and Kerry Mayfield
1450 Hwy. OO
Farmington, MO 63640

John and Kerry Mayfield
1450 Hwy. OO
Farmington, MO 63640

John and Kerry Mayfield
1450 Hwy. OO
Farmington, MO 63640

John and Kerry Mayfield
1450 Hwy. OO
Farmington, MO 63640

John and Kerry Mayfield
1450 Hwy. OO
Farmington, MO 63640

John and Kerry Mayfield
1450 Hwy. OO
Farmington, MO 63640

John and Kerry Mayfield
1450 Hwy. OO
Farmington, MO 63640

John and Kerry Mayfield
1450 Hwy. OO
Farmington, MO 63640

John and Kerry Mayfield
1450 Hwy. OO
Farmington, MO 63640

John and Kerry Mayfield
1450 Hwy. OO
Farmington, MO 63640

John and Kerry Mayfield
1450 Hwy. OO
Farmington, MO 63640

John and Kerry Mayfield
1450 Hwy. OO
Farmington, MO 63640

John and Kerry Mayfield
1450 Hwy. OO
Farmington, MO 63640

John and Kerry Mayfield
1450 Hwy. OO
Farmington, MO 63640

John and Kerry Mayfield
1450 Hwy. OO
Farmington, MO 63640

John and Kerry Mayfield
1450 Hwy. OO
Farmington, MO 63640

John and Kerry Mayfield
1450 Hwy. OO
Farmington, MO 63640

John and Kerry Mayfield
1450 Hwy. OO
Farmington, MO 63640

John and Kerry Mayfield
1450 Hwy. OO
Farmington, MO 63640

John and Kerry Mayfield
1450 Hwy. OO
Farmington, MO 63640

John and Kerry Mayfield
1450 Hwy. OO
Farmington, MO 63640

John and Kerry Mayfield
1450 Hwy. OO
Farmington, MO 63640

Experience Counts!

I specialize in...

Type Text Here Type Text Here Type Text Here Type Text Here

Type Text Here Type Text Here Type Text Here Type Text Here Type

Text Here Type Text Here

Experience

Type Text Here Type Text Here Type Text Here Type Text Here Type

Text Here Type Text Here Type Text Here

[Click here and type Organization Name and Duration]

[Title]
- [Type Text Here]
- [Type Text Here]
- [Type Text Here]

Education

[Click here and type University and Location]

Type Text Here Type Text Here Type Text Here Type Text Here Type Text Here Type Text Here

Type Text Here
- [Type Text Here]
- [Type Text Here]

[Click here and type University and Location]

Type Text Here Type Text Here Type Text Here Type Text Here Type Text Here Type Text Here

Type Text Here
- [Type Text Here]
- [Type Text Here]

Background and Personal Information

Type Text Here Type Text Here Type Text Here Type Text Here Type Text Here Type Text Here

Type Text Here
- [Type Text Here]
- [Type Text Here]

References

Available on Request

509 East Main St.
Park Hills, MO 63601
Office: 573-756-0077
Fax: 573-756-1336
Cell: 573-760-4220
Email: John@RealEstateTechGuy.com
Website: www.RealEstateTechGuy.com

John Mayfield GRI, CRB, ABR

Just Listed

Watch Your Golf Game Improve!

[Name of Condo Development] features 27- holes of golf
included with your condo association dues when you buy this
[#Bedrooms] bdrm. and *[#Baths]* bath
unit. Private setting with great shade trees, patio and more.
Over sized garage is ideal to store your golf cart too! To score
a par on this deal call *[Phone Number]* and ask for *[Listing
Agent]*. *[Listing Code Number]*

The following is an example of a shipping label that was created with HP REMA.

John Mayfield GRI, CRB, ABR

509 East Main St.
Park Hills, MO 63601

Office: 573-756-0077
Fax: 573-756-1336
Cell: 573-760-4220
Email: John@RealEstateTechGuy.com
Website: www.RealEstateTechGuy.com

«FirstName» «LastName»
«Address1» «Address2»
«City» «State» «PostalCode»«Next Record»

Index

$18.95 → $22.95